MW00882866

THE UNDERLYING CAUSES OF MENTAL ANOMALIES

The Basics That Psychiatrists and Psychologists Missed

Dr. Maxwell Nartey

© Copyright 2024, The American School of Symptometry, NFP. No part of this publication may be reproduced or transmitted in any form or by any means, electronic or mechanical, including photocopying, recording, or by any information storage and retrieval system without the written permission of The American School of Symptometry, NFP. Library of Congress copyright number Txu 1-621-370, Washington D.C.

Dedication

I dedicate this book to the nameless immortals who keep steering me away from the depressing culture of repetition, failures, and stagnation – the culture that keeps psychiatry stuck where it is with no new ideas to make this world a better place for all.

Acknowledgment

I am immensely grateful to my wife, Carolyn, and my children, Adelle, Belle, Rosalita, Kellie, and Harold, for their unwavering support and nurturing presence. Without their love and encouragement, I would not have had the peace of mind to dedicate 33 years to researching human behavior, conduct, attitude, traits, and personality to write this book.

My immediate family played an important role in this significant effort, culminating in a book that continues to provoke critical thinking about the direction of medical research and the basics of mental health, which psychiatrists and psychologists often overlook.

Table of Contents

About the Author

Dr. Maxwell Nartey, the maverick, makes things better.

The bachelor's degree and doctorate he obtained from Clayton College of Natural Health, the diploma in echocardiology obtained at the Medical Careers Institute in Chicago, and the postgraduate diploma in Homoeopathic Medicine obtained at the old British Institute of Homoeopathy in Middlesex, England, opened his eyes.

Then, the years of chromatographic analysis and research with Raman spectroscopy made him realize that mankind had been heading in the wrong direction for thousands of years. So, he decided to do something about it.

He conducted the kind of research that made him redirect mankind's attention to the cell, the unit of life; DNA; the gene-DNA-RNA realignment; the production of enzymes; and cell nourishment for cell protection and resilience. This was the route he chose to de-emphasize chaotic diets to fill the belly and emphasize the protection and well-being of our cells.

He invented scientific cooking, eating, and living based on verifiable science to separate cytotoxic substances from cell-friendly nutrients, thereby introducing a better and healthier way of life. This way of life is meant to protect our cells from harm and reinforce the importance of producing enzymes, activating them, and not denaturing or deactivating them to make optimal health possible.

By making the cells, the production of enzymes, and the circulation of cleaner oxygenated blood the focus of every health endeavor, Dr. Maxwell Nartey succeeded in making the well-being and protection of the cells as well as decreasing the number of blood impurities the pillars of Symptometric science, his invention.

For the first time in the history of the world, someone invented a science that caters to the needs of the cells and blood, and that person is Dr. Maxwell Nartey.

Symptometric science relegates disease to the back burner and thrusts the well-being of the cells to the forefront of human endeavor. It is this approach that enables Symptometric science to successfully address the needs of at least 85% of a person's cells, leaving medical science with the remaining 15%.

Additionally, Dr. Maxwell Nartey invented correlation diagnosis to fill the vacuum that electrodiagnosis and differential diagnosis created.

Correlation diagnosis makes a connection between the food a person has been eating and their ailments; a connection between the herbs or drugs a person has been taking and their diseases; a connection between the beverages a person has been consuming and their illnesses; a connection between a person's lifestyle and preferences and their diseases; and a connection between cell neglect and a person's diseases.

It is a correlation diagnosis that takes mysteries out of every illness, thereby confirming that to every anomaly, there is a cause, and this cause must be found and removed or neutralized. If not, the ailment will be chronic.

Dr. Nartey redefined health as the reward our cells bestow on the person who aligns the desires of their mind with the needs of their cells, making satisfying the needs of our cells, not our bellies, our topmost priority. His contribution to the advancement of knowledge in the world and ending stagnation in therapeutics by stimulating critical thinking could not have come at a better time.

He established the American School of Symptometry, NFP, to re-educate the miseducated and misinformed in matters of cellular health so that mature adults can now take full responsibility for their health.

Health is a personal responsibility, not the government's responsibility. His website, amsos.org, unfolds an impressive lineup of his accomplishments.

Introduction

Declining mental health has become such a worldwide concern that psychologists and psychiatrists are at a loss trying to solve this global problem.

According to a 2022 study conducted by Harvard, about 12.4% of pilots suffer from clinical depression. The study also revealed that approximately 4% of pilots have suicidal thoughts periodically. However, many pilots avoid seeking help from psychiatrists because they fear it may impact their careers negatively, even to the point of preventing them from continuing to fly.

Why do people with mental issues, especially depression, avoid psychiatrists? The answer is a psychiatric evaluation and diagnosis is a permanent stain on a person's record. It cannot be expunged because it is indelible, and it is indelible because, to psychiatrists, it is incurable.

Therefore, if an applicant is less than candid on their application about never receiving a psychiatric evaluation or diagnosis, and Human Resources finds out that they did, they will be terminated.

Addiction to alcohol, methamphetamine, psychedelic mushrooms, cocaine, marijuana, etc., will, at some point, cause depression. What causes an addiction in the first place?

Every addiction occurs because the person's diencephalon is ischemic (bloodless). Our hypothalamus, which hosts the pleasure centers, is in the diencephalon. Addictions occur because chemical receptors are in the ischemic pleasure centers.

Ischemia will spread from the diencephalon to the midbrain above it and then to the thalamus below it. Finally, it will spread to the brain stem and forebrain as plaque follows.

Acetylcholine is produced in the midbrain and forebrain. Serotonin is produced in the brain stem. Dopamine is produced in the midbrain and hypothalamus. If the midbrain and forebrain are ischemic, how can the brain cells in the midbrain and forebrain produce acetylcholine to end memory loss? They can't.

If the brain stem is ischemic, how can the cells in it produce serotonin to end or prevent depression? They can't. Do psychiatrists have what it takes to reverse ischemia in the brain stem, midbrain, and forebrain? No, they don't.

People have become addicted to all kinds of substances because their pleasure centers are ischemic and calcified.

I am discussing the basics of mental health from the

The Underlying Causes of Mental Anomalies

Symptometry perspective because the theories that are taught in psychiatry and psychology about the underlying causes of mental illness, brain disorders, and emotional disorders are too flawed to be rescued.

This book discusses the underlying causes of brain disorders, ranging from children to seniors. Regrettably, these are the basics that psychologists and psychiatrists keep missing.

Chapter One

From Darkness To Light

I remember vividly what we, as a class, were taught at the old British Institute of Homoeopathy in Middlesex, England. We were instructed to treat people according to their mental symptoms and idiosyncrasies.

Then, we were directed to use the Materia Medica to find the most suitable Hahnemannian product to match the person's mental symptoms and idiosyncrasies. We were assured that by treating the person's mental symptoms, the needs of all the different parts of their body would also be met. As a result, the person's many diseases would be cured.

I asked myself, how can the product for fear of thunder cure liver cirrhosis, which I had at the time? Also, how can the product for fear of thunder cure cold sensitivity, enlarged liver, sinusitis, nosebleeds, irritability, etc., which I had? My professor insisted that it was how classical homoeopathy requires that a person should be treated. This method, called repertorization, which is central to classical homoeopathy, did not help me one bit.

We were not taught anything about the cells, anatomy, DNA, enzymes, and blood. The word "Cell" was not mentioned once for the entire time I spent at the old British

Institute of Homoeopathy. All we were taught was the history of homoeopathy, the homoeopathic pharmacopeia which started with Cinchona officinalis, the application of similia similibus curantur, understanding and applying the three principles of homoeopathy to treatments; the doctrine of signatures, miasma, nosodes, sarcodes, vitalism, and repertorization.

After obtaining my diplomas, I discarded everything I was taught at the British Institute of Homoeopathy and decided to do things differently. I enrolled in Clayton College of Natural Health with the intent of learning a lot about the natural way of restoring health. Instead, what I was taught was not what I expected.

I had to start researching the cells, enzymes, salt, oxygenated blood, the pH rule, etc., to invent a different system and science because I refused to repeat my professors' mistakes and the mistakes of medical science.

Medical science ignores the plight or well-being of the cells and DNA as it plunges head-first into anatomy, physiology, pathology, vaccination, surgery, and pharmacology. This turns out to be the longest route to health without ever reaching its destination. Let me throw some logic into this discussion by asking two simple questions.

What produces the anatomical parts of the body that are

the focus of anatomists? It is the cells. What makes the anatomical parts function? It is salty, oxygenated blood full of automation, energy, and forces. Good salt releases more cations than anions. It is the cations from good salt that enable the cells to produce pathways for the production of mitochondrial energy; metabolic pathways, genetic pathways, and signal transduction pathways. It would be impossible to sustain life without these pathways. Hence, the importance of salt in human blood.

Therefore, skipping energy, forces, salt, automation, the cells, and blood and plunging straight into anatomy and physiology is a huge mistake that medical science will not stop making, and I am not going to repeat that mistake. Now, the facts.

I am writing about mental aberrations or anomalies for a reason. The reason is that psychiatrists and psychologists keep missing the fundamentals of mental health, and this writing discusses nothing but these fundamentals, starting with the cell that none of them mentions.

Nothing will work in a cell unless poisonless and salty oxygenated blood is in it. How does oxygenated blood get into the brain cells knowing full well that a cell measures only between 28 and 32 microns, which is less than one-fifth of a pinhead? First, I will discuss the different kinds of blood.

Chapter Two
Different Kinds Of Blood

Different kinds of blood should never be confused with different blood types. The blood-type concept is used to screen blood at the blood bank and for blood transfusion. Then, some individuals eat for their blood type (A, B, AB, and O), with O negative being the universal acceptor and donor.

Are people who eat for their blood type healthy? No, they are not in most instances. Why? Because they have dirty blood, blood loaded with poison, or blood loaded with toxins.

The formulator of Eat-4-Your Blood Type failed to realize that dirty blood is the problem, and diet, regardless of the kind of diet it is, can never remove blood impurities, and there are over 75 of such impurities.

Even though Symptometry's focus is the well-being of the cell and DNA, its work does not start with the cell. It starts with blood because to get to the cell, one must go through blood. What is a human cell without blood? Nothing.

The different kinds of blood refer to the quality of a

person's blood. Is the quality good or bad? Why is it good or bad? Bad blood denatures or deactivates enzymes. Also, there are fewer to no forces in bad blood.

There is blood in every cadaver, but the blood in cadavers has no force, making it bad blood. Good blood is the kind of blood that is loaded with a lot of force and automation. Additionally, it has nothing in it that denatures or deactivates enzymes. This is the difference between good and bad blood.

Would a blood test assist in classifying blood as good or bad? No. The hematologists who design blood tests have yet to come up with such a classification.

The five different kinds of blood are:

1. Poisonless oxygenated blood
2. De-oxygenated blood
3. Dirty blood
4. Blood loaded with poisons
5. Blood loaded with toxins, especially the toxins of streptococcus, diphtheria, or viruses.

Every person who is alive has blood in their arteries and veins, but what kind of blood is flowing through them? It is the kind of blood that flows through a person's arteries and ends up in their capillaries and cells, which determines whether they are healthy or not.

Therefore, the cells cannot produce essentials with what they don't have. If the cells cannot divide or if they divide but cannot produce certain essentials, it is because of the kind of blood they receive. This blood lacks forces and automation.

Let me take a moment to discuss the five kinds of blood, one or two of which flow through a person's arteries and capillaries.

1- Poisonless oxygenated blood is the best blood. It is loaded with automation and forces. A person who has this blood will be healthy for decades. Why? There is nothing in it that will denature or deactivate their enzymes. However, to produce it, the person should not have poison or halogen in their blood, and this requires knowing the sources of halogens and as many poisons as possible, especially the poisons in the foods people eat, such as lettuce, chocolate, and nuts.

2- Deoxygenated blood is venous blood. Venous blood flows to the heart while oxygenated blood flows in the opposite direction, meaning from the heart through the arteries to the organs, tissues, membranes, and cells. Deoxygenated blood has less oxygen. For health, a person needs more, not less, oxygen.

3- Dirty blood is clotty blood. It causes capillary occlusion, resulting in ischemia (bloodlessness) or a stroke.

4- Blood loaded with poisons is the blood in individuals who eat chaotically, allowing poisons to flow side by side with oxygen in their arteries and capillaries, sometimes limiting the availability of oxygen to their cells.

There is lactucopicrin in lettuce, prussic acid in nuts, theobromine in coffee and chocolate, theophylline in all teas, cyanide in corn, pears, plums, and lima beans, patulin in mushrooms, bromine in sea salt, solanine in tomatoes, potatoes, eggplant, and so on. Unless a person produces specific enzymes to neutralize these poisons, there will always be poison in their blood.

Poisoned blood destroys albumins and globulins; it causes chronic fatigue in general and fatigue after eating, aches and pains, irritability, anger, blisters, ulcers, lack of focus or concentration, and a short attention span. Why? Because poison destroys the circulators and deactivates the enzyme that accelerates the production of neurotransmitters.

Also, poisoned blood facilitates mutation to cause cancer.

Why do some individuals have difficulty breathing? They have difficulty breathing because they lack oxygen even though the water they drink, the air they breathe, and the foods they eat have oxygen. Unless they produce enzymes to neutralize these poisons, the poisons will keep eliminating oxygen from their lungs.

The Underlying Causes of Mental Anomalies

Every person who has an infection will automatically have poisoned blood because microbial toxins deactivate enzymes and make blood filthy. Antibiotics and antiviral drugs can kill the pathogens, but they never touch the toxins that pathogens leave in the person's blood.

Then, there are poisons from the food most people eat. These poisons combine with microbial toxins to make it impossible for the cells to self-correct, self-adjust, self-cleanse, self-protect, and self-perpetuate. These food poisons were discussed earlier.

Poison deactivates enzymes, and if the enzymes called kinase and cyclin that divide the stem cells in the red bone marrow are deactivated, the stem cells will not divide to produce hundreds of T cells, B cells, basophils, neutrophils, monocytes, eosinophils, etc. to prevent or stop an infection. This is how pathogens outnumber white blood cells 4,000 to 1, and viruses or fungi outnumber interferons 6,000 to 1 to cause an infection.

The idea that herpes is incurable, HIV is incurable, etc., is being spread by professionals who studied medical science, not symptometric science.

Medical science never discusses how poisons and toxins denature and deactivate enzymes because they do not discuss enzymes. All they discuss are pathology and pharmaceutical drugs, and these drugs have alkyl. What does alkyl do? It eliminates hydrogen. Hydrogen is essential to the cells.

5- Blood loaded with toxins. Toxins and poisons have a similar effect on our enzymes. They denature or deactivate them.

For example, the toxins of streptococcus and diphtheria cause Raynaud's disease, which is a person's inability to stay warm. In Raynaud's disease, the person cannot produce enough body heat to keep warm. Why? Because the toxins of streptococcus and diphtheria block heat transfer from adipose (fat) tissue to muscle tissue.

If streptococcus is present in a pregnant woman's blood, chances are, she will pass on the bacterium to her baby, causing the child to have streptococcus in their blood. I am explaining why babies are born with streptococcus in their blood and how the streptococcus in the child's blood will cause susceptibility to styes, boils, abscesses, cold sensitivity, cold feet, cold hands, cold ears, and weak immunity.

Dr. Edward Jenner invented vaccination in 1798 to drastically reduce infant mortality. Why were children dying from smallpox, diphtheria, pertussis, tetanus, mumps, etc.? They had weak immunity. It was the presence of streptococcus in the children's blood that lowered their immunity to the point where their white blood cells and interferons were worthless.

12

Unfortunately, Dr. Edward Jenner, Dr. Louis Pasteur, Dr. Lister, and other bacteriologists never studied the source of weak immunity.

According to microbiology, streptococcus produces and releases ten toxins, which are:

1. Streptokinase
2. Streptolysins
3. Hemolysin
4. Hyaluronidase
5. Deoxyribonuclease
6. Exfoliating toxin
7. M. Proteins
8. Leucocidins
9. NADase, and
10. Glycosyltransferase.

Streptococcus is predominantly a skin bacterium. It protects the skin from airborne pathogens. However, this protection depends on our ability to keep our skin acidic, meaning at a pH of 6.5.

Why use soaps that alter the pH of the skin? It is because the pH rule has been altered that streptococcus has no other choice than to invade the tissues and cause an infection or a boil.

In the tonsils, streptococcus may cause tonsillitis. In the

throat, it may cause laryngitis, pharyngitis, sore throat, glossitis, hoarseness, swollen throat, pain in the throat, difficulty swallowing, or the inability to swallow. In the eyelids, it may cause styes.

Do individuals know what the pH rule is? No, they don't. How does streptococcus migrate from the hands or skin to the eyes, ears, mouth, throat, and vagina? Then, how does it migrate from the mouth or vagina to the bloodstream? People should be aware that streptococcus is almost always on our hands and under our fingernails. These are lessons that should be taught in hygiene but are not.

Do people wash their hands with soap before they rub their eyes or eyelids? Most of them don't. Do women wash their hands before they masturbate? No, they don't. Do people wash their hands and fruits before they eat fruits? No, most of them don't.

Streptococcus and staphylococcus are not our enemies. They enforce the pH rule and good hygiene. Therefore, violating these rules will cause an infection, a boil, an abscess, and, in the worst-case scenario, death. Their toxins may slam shut the airways to cause death.

People want to have healthy longevity, but how can they have healthy longevity if they know nothing about the pH rule, the rules of health, how to produce enzymes, enzyme activation, enzyme deactivation, the production of hormones and neurotransmitters, etc.?

Per the Gerontology Research Group, there are about 400 supercentenarians, meaning people who have lived for over 110 years. Even though they are supercentenarians, they are not in the best of health. Some cannot hear, are blind, have Raynaud syndrome, are almost always constipated, cannot digest food, have swallowing problems, are bedridden, do not know what day it is, cannot remember what they had for breakfast, are toothless, etc. This is not healthy longevity by Symptometry's standards. They are hanging to life by a thread. Are these examples to emulate? No, they are not.

Living "by the grace of God" is not what Symptometry advocates. We want to continue to live in an optimally healthy body because we mastered the pH rule, the rules of health and hygiene, the iron rule, natural law, etc.

Then, we follow our intuition, and we know how to produce enzymes, activate them, and not denature or deactivate them, etc., and all these are possible thanks to Symptometric science, not medical science.

Living healthily on this hostile, predatory, and toxic planet is no joke. Nevertheless, we, in Symptometry, found a way to do it. God gave us a brain, and we are using it to the best of our ability. Medical science will be there when we need it, but when it comes to cellular health, we prefer

Symptometric science because it also takes care of mental health.

What do psychiatrists and psychologists keep missing? They keep missing the quality of the person's blood, how blood gets into the brain cells and neural stem cells, and how the cells use nutrients and resources to produce enzymes, neurotransmitters, hormones, and neurons to make a person mentally and emotionally healthy.

Chapter Three

How Blood Moves From the Arteries to the Cells

Diffusion and facilitated diffusion are the processes that enable blood to get from the cerebral capillaries into the cells of the different brain components. Then, the filtration force in the capillaries pushes oxygenated blood into each brain cell, allowing the nucleus, the cytoplasm, and each cellular organelle to function.

When examining a diseased organ, it is observed that some spots are discolored, meaning the cells in these areas have not had oxygenated blood in months, if not years.

The question is, why the discoloration or the presence of plaque or calcification? The answer is the filtration force that pushes oxygenated blood from the capillaries into the brain cells was either weak or non-existent. Without blood, brain cells with permeable membranes will deteriorate. This makes the lack of poisonless oxygenated blood in the brain cells one of the underlying causes of mental anomalies.

Brain cells need blood, and it is capillaries that provide them with blood and oxygen. What is the importance of oxygen to the brain cells? Oxygen maintains the life principle, and the life principle is the exchange principle. We are all alive because of the exchange/life principle.

Oxygen sustains the life principle by providing the force that sustains life, electron exchange, and gas exchange (oxygen and carbon dioxide) in the lung's air sacs.

The blood that is provided to the brain gets into the brain cell's cytoplasm and nucleus. The organelles in the cytoplasm use salty oxygenated blood to produce whatever is necessary to enable the brain to function optimally.

Some of the essentials that ribosomal RNA in the brain cells and other cells must produce to enable the brain to function optimally include:

1. Enzymes (permeases, kinase and cyclin, DNA polymerase, RNA polymerase, isomerases, cell cleaners, poison busters, acid busters, etc.)
2. Myelinated and unmyelinated neurons. They form white and gray matter, arachnoid mater, pia mater, and dura mater.
3. Neuropeptides.
4. Sound filters
5. Light filters
6. Image stabilizers
7. Image normalizers
8. Image filters
9. Idea producers

10. Dopamine
11. Norepinephrine
12. Melatonin
13. Epinephrine
14. Myelin and
15. Acetylcholine

Therefore, as long as oxygenated blood is available, the brain cells will not have an anomaly, meaning they will be healthy. Why? Because the brain cells, neural stem cells, and glial cells will divide to achieve their objectives.

What do glial cells do? They clean the neurons to prevent sludge that gets stuck on them from slowing them down.

Neural stem cells produce neurons by the billions. Why? Because neurons do not divide to replace themselves. It is because they fade away after every neuronal connection that the neural stem cells must produce a new wave of neurons, usually every 24 hours.

Brain cells are like nerve cells, skin cells, muscle cells, etc., because they divide. It is because they divide that their ribosomal RNAs produce enzymes, neuropeptides, dopamine, sound filters, sound blockers, image blockers, light filters, image stabilizers, image normalizers, and image filters while neurons connect with other neurons to produce fresh ideas, and solutions, and create new possibilities, concepts, and opportunities.

Then, neurons team up with electrolytes and neurotransmitters to enable a person to achieve several objectives at the same time, such as walking in a straight line and chewing gum; thinking and talking on the phone; judging distance and making decisions or assumptions; reasoning, remembering, planning, organizing, strategizing, and prioritizing objectives without being distracted. Finally, neurons enable a person to learn and acquire a skill or several skills so they can re-invent themselves. What can we do without neurons? Nothing. It is neurons and neurotransmitters that make us excel in whatever we do.

The other glands in the brain, such as the pineal gland, the pituitary gland, and the pituitary-hypothalamus complex, perform functions that turn the brain into the command center of the entire human body. For example, the pineal gland produces melatonin. It is melatonin that makes us sleep restfully and soundly, making us shift automatically from the conscious state to the subconscious state. This shift, which should last between 4 and 6 hours, enables billions of our cells to clean themselves, repair themselves, and readjust to new circumstances while the neural stem cells produce a new wave of neurons.

Acetylcholine makes us alert and runs our conscious state most of the time, while melatonin runs our subconscious state for 4 to 6 hours. In other words, they run shifts. As one ends its shift, the other begins its shift, and all this is possible because neurons, electrolytes, and neurotransmitters work around the clock.

Now, the reverse. What will the reverse look like if oxygenated blood is not in the brain? The reverse will be chaotic because neurofibrillary plaque will replace oxygenated blood, thereby shutting down one gland after another and one brain component after another. It is the subsequent shutting down of the brain components that will cause various mental anomalies, personality disorders, and emotional disturbances.

What does plaque do? It distorts a person's view of life and the world, causing them to engage in anti-social behavior and reprehensible conduct.

What makes plaque replace oxygenated blood in most parts of the brain? The answer is capillary collapse, capillary occlusion, and ischemia. This is why every person who has mental or cognitive problems has plaque in their brain.

Chapter Four
Capillaries

Brain cells get their supplies from the capillaries, not from the arteries. It is the brain and other organs that get their supplies from the arteries. Here comes the question.

If there are no capillaries to supply blood to the brain cells, glial cells, and neural stem cells, how can these cells divide? They can't.

If neural stem cells do not divide, neurons will not be produced, and a person who can't produce neurons won't be able to:

1. Think properly
2. Discipline themselves
3. Control their behavior
4. Control their bad habits
5. Control their thirst
6. Control their appetite
7. Control their anger
8. React calmly to most situations
9. Rationalize their thoughts and observations properly, resulting in unnecessary suspicions and conspiracies
10. Plan
11. Coordinate

12. Organize

13. Strategize

14. Prioritize

15. Do arithmetic

16. Use reflexes

17. Understand

18. Analyze

19. Weigh the pros and cons of an action

20. Study or learn

21. Judge distance

22. Set goals

23. Be determined to achieve a goal

24. Reason rationally

25. Write in paragraphs

26. Think about the future

27. Have a relationship with a person other than their parent

28. Drive responsibly

29. Obey rules and regulations, resort to peaceful means to settle differences, and change what needs to be changed without violence

A person who has a neurofibrillary plaque in their association areas, hippocampus, cerebral cortex, limbic system, etc., will:

1. Become emotionless, cold-hearted, and lack empathy

2. Become defiant of authority
3. Develop the inability to make sound decisions
4. Become an extremist
5. Become a fanatic
6. Become vindictive
7. Become hateful
8. Easily lose the thread of a conversation
9. Use profanities
10. Develop the inability to produce ideas
11. Become forgetful
12. Talk in a disconnected manner
13. Suffer from aphasia
14. Have a bad omen (feeling that something unpleasant is going to happen)
15. Become headstrong, obstinate, opinionated, etc.
16. Hear voices because they cannot produce voice and sound filters
17. Hallucinate because they cannot produce image stabilizers, image filters, light filters, and image normalizers
18. Not be able to plan, coordinate, organize, strategize, do arithmetic, use reflexes, analyze, understand, judge distance, weigh the pros and cons of an action, study or learn, acquire a skill, set goals, reason rationally, have a relationship with a person other than their parent, think about the future, follow rules and regulations, etc.

The Underlying Causes of Mental Anomalies

The above are the complete opposites of a person who produces neurons, neuropeptides, and neurotransmitters and consumes electrolytes.

Also, it is important to emphasize that neurofibrillary plaque distorts a person's view of life and the world, causing them to justify:

1. Mischief
2. Arson
3. Stealing (shoplifting, bank robbery, armed robbery, pickpocketing, etc.)
4. Breaking into cars, homes, etc.
5. Murder
6. Hurting the person who offended them
7. Kidnapping
8. Rape
9. Cruelty to animals
10. Cruelty to a child
11. Abusive behavior
12. Impulsivity
13. Indifference to the plight of others
14. Daydreaming or absent-mindedness
15. Belligerence
16. Hatred for other human beings
17. Dislike for girls and women
18. Dislike for boys and men
19. Dislike for homosexuals, transgenders, etc.

20. Dislike for pets
21. Tolerance of filth, clutter, etc.
22. Opportunism
23. Manipulation
24. Cheating
25. Exploitation
26. Bad manners
27. Bad behavior
28. Reprehensible conduct
29. Child molestation
30. Abuse of seniors
31. Lack of morals, etc.

Arresting social misfits and people who engage in disorderly conduct and jailing them or prosecuting and imprisoning them will not remove the source of their mental aberrations. Even counseling them will not help.

Many police officers have argued that keeping criminals in prison where they belong keeps the streets and communities safe. What they fail to realize is that keeping some criminals in jail or prison, which is good, also allows a new crop of criminals to replace those who are in prison. This is called solving a problem to create a new problem, thereby swinging from crisis to crisis.

It is Symptometry's observation that the more jails and prisons are built, the more prison guards, police officers, court officers, and parole officers are trained and paid, the greater the number of people who engage in disorderly conduct, thereby creating a vicious cycle of misconduct.

This vicious cycle of misconduct that can easily be stopped has been allowed to continue for centuries if not for thousands of years. It can be stopped not by the police but by focusing on the new generation's brain health, starting with Symptometry's pregnancy management program, post-partum care, scientific cooking, scientific eating, and scientific living.

As the old generation of misfits and mentally deranged individuals fade away, a healthier crop of new and young citizens with healthier brains will emerge to replace the old generation.

Symptometry is proposing, through this discussion, a permanent solution to the mental health crises in the world.

Chapter Five
Capillary Collapse

A capillary with a diameter of 8-10 micrometers is so tiny that all the red blood cells, platelets, and white blood cells must file through it in a single line. Suppose capillary stenosis (narrowing) restricts the number of red blood cells that file through the capillary; what will happen to the cells at the other end of the organ or membrane? They will not get water, nutrients, electrolytes, etc.

Therefore, capillaries are not only thin; they can be stenosed, and they are also fragile. They are so fragile that they collapse easily.

What causes the collapse of the capillaries? Several factors cause their collapse. Such factors include:

1. Changes in atmospheric pressure
2. Higher altitude
3. Suffocation
4. Deep sea pressure from the weight of the water above a person who is 5,000 feet below the surface
5. Sudden change in the weather
6. Emotional trauma, as a person with a broken heart
7. Physical trauma, as experienced by a person who has received a blow to the head

8. Grief trauma, as experienced by a mother grieving the death of her child
9. Disappointment
10. Stress
11. Anger
12. Tension
13. Friction, etc.

We travel, we lose a loved one or friend, we relocate to a different neighborhood, we are disappointed, we grieve, we are sad, etc. These are the realities of life that cause tension in our bodies, friction in our relationships, and stress. At the same time, these factors cause thousands of our capillaries to collapse.

We may appear to be calm visually and externally, but internally, we are not all that calm. We are heartbroken, and things are not going well because thousands of our capillaries have collapsed, setting the stage for anomalies in different parts of our bodies.

People who claim they are healthy turn out not to be so healthy in many areas of their bodies. Their feet sweat, they itch here and there, they have dry mouth or halitosis, they are gassy, they have dry hair, dry skin, dry eyes, hemorrhoids, their legs feel heavy when they walk, etc. These are just a few of the dozens of anomalies people who claim they are healthy have.

If the collapse of thousands of capillaries deprives the association areas in the brain of oxygenated blood, the following may occur:

1. Agoraphobia (panic attack when overcome by the feeling of being trapped in a tiny space like in a submarine, a closet, etc.)
2. Panic attacks
3. Crowd anxiety
4. Nervousness
5. Fear of the dark
6. Inability to bear the smallest amount of pain or oversensitivity to pain. Pregnant women who have this problem prefer C-section to normal vaginal delivery, making their babies susceptible to neurological disorders.
7. Lack of confidence
8. Timidity
9. Shyness
10. Indecision
11. Fear of the crowd
12. Fear of strangers
13. Feeling of insecurity
14. Fear of heights
15. Fear of the unknown, for this reason, cannot travel too far from home
16. Fear of looking down from high above
17. Stage fright

18. Examination anxiety
19. Fear of failing
20. Hesitancy
21. Confusion
22. Fear of being touched
23. Fear of being approached by a male
24. Fear of being approached by a female
25. Fear of getting sick
26. Fear of dying when seriously sick
27. Fear of going to a physician, causing blood pressure to spike
28. Fear of heart disease, especially at night
29. Oversensitivity to noise
30. Tendency to talk in one's sleep

There are different faculties in the brain, such as the thalamus, diencephalon, limbic system, etc. Therefore, for a person to be mentally and emotionally balanced throughout their lives so they can make sound decisions, poisonless oxygenated blood must flow to every part of their brain, and this can only be done by reversing capillary collapse.

Criminals and social misfits are either behind bars or in front of bars, meaning they have not yet been arrested, jailed, prosecuted, or imprisoned. As long as people have capillaries that have collapsed in their brains, we should not expect peace and security to prevail on this planet any time soon.

If capillaries collapse in certain parts of the brain, sooner or later, the capillaries in the glands, such as the pineal gland, hypothalamus, and pituitary gland, where hormones are produced, will also collapse. Then, the capillaries in the sweat glands, salivary glands, sebaceous glands, lachrymal glands, digestive glands, and other glands may also collapse.

Finally, the capillaries that supply blood to the sphincters, veinous valves, heart valves, muscles, nerves, blood vessels, etc., will also collapse.

The point I am making is that if the capillaries that are in the brain collapse, the capillaries that are in the different parts of the body will also collapse. This serial collapse of capillaries has nothing to do with a person's age. It is just a fact of life. In other words, this is just how capillaries are.

The weather, the tension in a bad relationship, trauma, sleeping on a bad bed, a blow to the body, etc., cause the collapse of dozens or hundreds of our capillaries.

Are we going to accept that the capillaries in our bodies collapsed and should remain collapsed? No. We must do something to reverse such collapse to stay healthy.

We are in the 21st century, and for thousands if not millions of years, no one ever mentioned capillary collapse, capillary occlusion, and weak filtration force as the underlying cause of all anomalies in a person. Now, Symptometric science is making a difference by being the first science to attribute anomalies to capillary collapse or capillary occlusion, resulting in ischemia and the formation of plaque in the brain. Let me, at this point, elaborate on capillary occlusion.

Chapter Six
Capillary Occlusion

There are over 70 impurities in human blood. These include blood clots, fat globules, bone spurs, balls of debris, recombinants, and sludge, and the capillaries that circulate blood to the cells are so tiny that some of them are invisible to the unaided eye.

For example, an ophthalmologist must use an ophthalmoscope to check the eye but to check the blood vessels at the back of the eye (fundus), they must do a fundoscopy.

To find out how tiny our capillaries are, it is important to rely on fundoscopy because it is fundoscopy that reveals how tiny the capillaries in our eyes are and if blood impurities have blocked circulation to the optic nerve, cones, rods, macula, etc. Therefore, it is fundoscopy that can shed light on the reason a person has dim vision.

The same can be said of the capillaries found in our fingers, toes, palms, and mucus membranes in different parts of the body: ears, lips, tongue, inner cheeks, face, etc. Occlusion can cause the same problem that capillary collapse causes, which is ischemia (bloodlessness) with devastating consequences.

A person who successfully eliminates a significant amount of garbage from their blood will be healthier than a person who does not. This is because instead of having three sources of anomalies (capillary collapse, capillary occlusion, and weak filtration force), they will have two (capillary collapse and weak filtration force). Then, they will be radiantly healthier if they avoid poisons or neutralize them.

Is it easy to be healthy on this planet? No, it is not. This is because the knowledge that can help a person become healthy can only be obtained through Symptometry. None of what I am teaching in this book is known to the public or to those who studied medicine, Chinese traditional medicine, acupuncture, chiropractic, naturopathy, herbalism, and Ayurveda.

Are Symptometry's teachings secret? No, they are not. A person who studies advanced Symptometry will have access to them.

Infections, inflammation, tissue degeneration, and discoloration occur only in bloodless areas. This is not taught in pathology.

Teaching cellular health in this manner helps explain why Hahnemannian products work. They have enough thermal energy, electrical energy, and magnetic energy to revitalize the collapsed capillaries, ionize occlusions, and increase the filtration force. It is the combination of these three measures that allows the circulation of oxygenated blood to resume. Once the cells get what they have been waiting for, they will divide again. Then, once cell division resumes, cell self-correction will take place.

This teaching is so simple, down to earth, and to the point that it demystifies and debunks everything we were taught about inflammation, infections, low bone density, fevers, cramps, spasms, etc.

Most of us know that pharmaceutical drugs have side effects, but no one knows *how* they cause side effects. The same can be said of herbs. This book explains why.

Some pharmaceutical drugs are excellent for emergency treatment, but after they have stabilized a person's condition, a natural and scientific method must be used to facilitate cell self-correction, self-repair, self-protection, and self-perpetuation, and this method is Symptometry.

Chapter Seven
Capillary Health

What are the criteria for determining the health of a person's capillaries? A person's nails and eyes reflect the state of their capillaries.

Why the nails and the eyes? Because we cannot see a person's liver, kidneys, pancreas, adrenal gland, etc., to evaluate the state of their capillaries, we can see their eyes and nails. This is why the eyes and nails give the most accurate assessment of what is happening to the capillaries in a person's organs and glands.

Does the person have eye disorders? Does the person have nail disorders? They do not have to answer these questions; just look at their eyes and nails and draw your conclusion.

Does the person wear glasses to drive or to read the fine print? If they do not wear glasses to drive, then they have healthier capillaries than a person who does. Does the person drive at night with glasses or without glasses? If they wear glasses to drive at night, they have a capillary problem.

There are other eye disorders such as dry eyes, burning eyes, itchy eyes, pain in the eye, glaucoma, floaters, cataracts, dim vision, seeing double, seeing green, yellow, red, or white that indicate more serious eye problems than just wearing glasses. However, I will discuss them at another time. Now, let me discuss the nails.

Does the person have thick nails, split nails, curved nails, deformed nails, hangnails, infected hangnails, chalky cuticles, a line in the nails, white spots in the nails, a lunula (crescent in the nails), nails that have fallen off, in-growing nails, soft nails, dark nails, discolored nails, ridged nails, brittle nails, crumbling nails, flaws in the nails, or nails that are sore or painful? If the answer to any of the above questions is yes, it means the person has a serious capillary problem.

The condition of a person's nails before going for a manicure or pedicure says a lot about that person's capillary health. Unfortunately, these telltale signs are often ignored or covered up with nail polish. In Symptometry, they say a lot about the person's widespread ischemia.

It is ischemia that causes nail and eye anomalies, but we have no control over how long our capillaries can last. As was discussed earlier, disappointment or grieving the sudden loss of a loved one can cause thousands of capillaries to collapse in the brain, eyes, kidneys, liver, nails, scrotum, uterus, bladder, stomach, etc.

Capillaries are the tiniest blood vessels and they are everywhere in the human body. They are so delicate that they can rupture, collapse, or become occluded at any time.

An optometrist or ophthalmologist's equipment called a retinoscope, a retinal camera, a visual view analyzer, or an ophthalmoscope can help describe how tiny these capillaries are. Most of them look like lines drawn with a sharp pencil.

Imagine a blood clot in some of these capillaries that look like pencil lines. This blood clot will cut off circulation, say, to the optic nerve, optic chiasma, 3,000 rods, 5,000 cones, the macula, etc., to cause ischemia-related eye disorders. The same can be said of a blood clot cutting off circulation to the cells of the fingernails or toenails, part of the nephrons in the kidneys, part of the liver, spleen, eardrum, ascending colon, sigmoid, etc.

I am not referring to the big blood clots that cause DVT (deep vein thrombosis). I am referring to the tiny blood clots that are almost always in our blood, and women can see them in their menstrual blood. Pharmaceutical drugs cannot dissolve these tiny clots.

Billions of individuals, including children, are constipated. Do they know why? No, they don't. They are constipated because their colon capillaries are either occluded or have collapsed. However, instead of getting an ionizer from Symptometry to ionize the clots in their colon's capillaries, they use herbs or stool softeners to facilitate bowel movement. The bad news is that their colon's capillaries will remain occluded, meaning the underlying cause of their constipation will not be addressed.

Can an optometrist's eye drops reverse capillary occlusion, causing dry eyes, cataracts, glaucoma, burning eyes, dim vision, seeing double, seeing half of an object, etc.? No, they cannot because they are molecules. Molecules do not penetrate the cells unless the person produces enzymes called permeases.

Why can't a person swallow food or even water? Visit the intensive care units and the critical care units of hospitals and see patients with tubes in their noses, throats, or stomachs because they cannot swallow. They cannot swallow anything because the capillaries that circulate oxygenated blood to the cells of their swallowing muscles are either occluded or have collapsed.

Then, their stomachs are distended because they cannot produce enzymes to digest the liquefied food and water that they are fed through tubes. These patients are having this terrible experience because their capillaries are either occluded or have collapsed, causing ischemia. Finally, their ischemic glands cannot produce digestive enzymes, causing fermentation, bloating, gassiness, and massive congestion.

I am devoting more time to the discussion of the pencil lines, aka capillaries, because acupuncturists, physicians, surgeons, chiropractors, naturopaths, herbalists, Ayurveda practitioners, and Chinese medical practitioners cannot do anything about capillary collapse, capillary occlusion, and weak filtration force.

Acupuncturists talk about circulation. Then, what do they do? They use acupuncture needles to redirect circulation along the meridians, leaving the capillaries occluded and ischemia in place. They are circumventing the problem.

No one on this earth will be healthy in any part of their body unless they can reverse capillary occlusion, capillary collapse, weak filtration force, and ischemia. Veganism, vegetarianism, eating raw fish, raw meat, only fruits, mostly nuts, or for one's blood type, etc., is inconsistent with the way our cells operate. It is inconsistent because the plight of the pencil lines (capillaries) is left unattended, causing widespread ischemia throughout the body.

All these diets and dietary supplements will add more garbage to the cells that have already been crushed. By the way, most dieters are not aware that they are suffering from the consequences of widespread ischemia, as evidenced by the quality of their nails, eyes, saliva, etc.

Nail polish does not just enhance beauty. It is also meant to mask the flaws in a woman's fingernails and toenails. Unfortunately, it cannot mask the flaws that are in the woman's eyes, glands, organs, etc. Instead of masking these flaws, Symptometry recommends turning these flaws into a warning of worse things to come and taking corrective measures before it is too late.

Chapter Eight

Ischemia

Ischemia is bloodlessness, and it is caused by capillary occlusion and capillary collapse, which leave all the cells at the other end without blood and, by extension, without water, salt, oxygen, and nutrients.

What will a retina without blood become? Nothing, there will be anomalies in it. What will a macula without blood become? Nothing, macular degeneration will occur. What will nails without blood become? They will have anomalies. What will a heart without blood become? It will become so weak that it will collapse, leading to heart failure.

What will a hippocampus without blood become? It will become a cesspool of brain disorders. What will a cerebral cortex without blood become? It will become the source of personality disorders. These examples make ischemia the source of countless anomalies, including gangrene.

All kinds of therapeutics have emerged without saying anything about the capillaries. This is sad indeed. The anatomy books mention ischemia without linking it to anomalies in the body.

Symptometry's objective is to address the needs of the

cells and DNA. Still, these needs cannot be addressed unless ischemia, capillary collapse, capillary occlusion, and weak filtration force are mentioned, explained, and reversed.

Two factors cause ischemia:

1) capillary collapse and

2) capillary occlusion.

Therefore, ischemia can happen at any time in any part of the body.

The following cause capillary occlusion, leaving the cells in different parts of the body without blood and oxygen, and by extension, without nutrients and resources:

1. Embolus (a wandering blood clot that gets stuck and cuts off circulation).
2. Concretions (plaque, lithiasis, calculi, tophus, gravel, stone, sand, etc.).
3. Fat globule.
4. Ball of debris.
5. Pile of sludge.
6. Deep sea pressure that rolls debris, concretions, and fat globules into a ball to cause an occlusion.
7. Extremely high altitudes where atmospheric pressure or cabin pressure rolls blood impurities into a ball to cause an occlusion.

8. Emotional traumas: loss of a child, grieving, disappointment, loss of luggage or high-value items, loss of a home, a job, etc.

9. Physical traumas including concussions and blows to the body. No one suffers from such traumas as kickboxers, boxers, football players, people who fall from a horse or are gorged by a bull, people who fall from a story building, or people who are stoned or hit with bricks.

10. Extremely cold temperatures. Why drink iced water and cold items? Why eat ice cream, popsicles, etc.? People who fall into partly frozen lakes suffer from hypothermia and frostbite. Extreme cold turns debris and concretions into a ball to cause capillary occlusion.

11. Extremely hot temperatures. Sunstroke during a heat wave or being locked in a shipping container on a hot day for hours. Extreme heat turns debris and concretions into a ball to cause an occlusion.

How can a person who does not have the most suitable Hahnemannian products remove these above-mentioned causal factors, and reverse capillary occlusion to end ischemia in their body? They cannot.

Diet, regardless of the kind of diet it is, will only add more concretions, fat globules, balls of debris, sludge, etc., to what is already in the cells. As a result, ischemia will not be reversed.

Hot water application indeed adds thermal energy to the tissues, but it does not end ischemia. It is the tissue as a whole that benefits from the hot water application, not the filtration force in the capillaries.

What do physicians have for ischemia? Nothing. Herbalists and naturopaths do not even know what ischemia is. Billions of individuals are not aware that it is widespread ischemia that causes most of their anomalies.

Then, physicians classify certain individuals as "terminally ill, people with chronic diseases, or mystery diseases". Nothing could be further from the truth. The fact is, nothing will work in a cell unless oxygenated blood is in it. Why? The answer is that our cells cannot function without nutrients, and blood supplies nutrients and resources. Let me at this point discuss the weak filtration force and how it contributes to many anomalies.

Weak Filtration Force

It is a filtration force using a lot of power, strength, and pressure to push plasma and red blood cells through the capillaries that look like pencil lines.

What weakens the filtration force in the capillaries, preventing the cells from getting oxygen, salt, and nutrients?

It is pharmaceutical drugs, poisons, toxic alkaloids, tumorigens, carcinogens, etc., that weaken the filtration force in the capillaries.

Therefore, if the cells can't get blood full of force, power, strength, nutrients, oxygen, etc., DNA and the chromosomes in the nucleus will also not get the nutrients and resources that blood circulates.

Calling diseases chromosomal disorders masks the source of the chromosomal disorder. In truth, a person who regularly has nutrients and resources in their cells will never have a chromosomal disorder.

Chapter Nine

Brain Injury

I decided to discuss brain injury because the doctors of sports medicine and sports medicine specialists have never discussed it coherently.

The brain is nothing but mushy grayish matter, which, when examined microscopically, does not contain fat; but contains countless blood vessels crisscrossing a vast terrain. Cerebral capillaries and arteries are extremely fragile and will develop an aneurysm if they are not strengthened.

Brain injury or brain trauma caused by a head-on collision, banging the head against a hard surface, a blow or several blows to the head, or falling head-first from a story building should never be taken lightly because it can be a life-changing accident. Here is why.

Not only will the brain trauma smash the neuron/neurotransmitter complex, but it will also disrupt many pathways in the brain, cause the collapse and occlusion of many cerebral capillaries, and disrupt the head-to-toe connections. Cerebral palsy is a classic example of what happens to a person who suffers a brain injury, meaning the neural stem cells that produce neurons atrophy, and many cerebral capillaries collapse.

How did a person's mental illness begin? Many individuals have no recollection of how their mental illness or brain disorder began. There are three ways that mental aberrations begin. They can begin as a) head trauma, b) capillary occlusion, or c) capillary collapse resulting in ischemia.

A person can have poison-less oxygenated blood flowing through their cerebral capillaries, but if their capillaries have collapsed or are occluded, their excellent blood will not go anywhere. As a result, ischemia will occur, and neurofibrillary plaque will fill many parts of the brain, causing chronic headaches, seizures, or visual disturbances.

The vasomotor center that controls the skeletal muscles and smooth muscles is in the cerebellum (back of the head). The cardiac center that controls the heart is in the cerebellum, and the respiratory center that controls breathing is also in the cerebellum.

Then, dopamine and acetylcholine are produced in the midbrain, and serotonin is made in the brain stem. Are the capillaries that provide the cells in these brain components with nutrients still open, or have they collapsed or become occluded?

Boxers, kickboxers, football players, and many others who suffered brain trauma have not stopped having mental problems, and this is because of capillary collapse, capillary occlusion, ischemia, and the formation of neurofibrillary plaque in their brains.

Do they come to Symptometry to reverse what is happening to them? No, they go to psychiatrists, physical therapists, and counselors who keep ischemia and neurofibrillary plaque in place.

By keeping cell neglect in place, their brain problem will spread to the rest of their body, causing neurological problems, muscle spasms and cramps, bone problems, joint problems, heart problems, ambulatory problems, gastrointestinal problems, etc. This is how what happens to the brain will sooner or later occur in different parts of the body, lending credence to the saying, "As above, so below".

Read chapter 12 of this book to see what happens when neurofibrillary plaque replaces oxygenated blood in the brain. The consequences are devastating.

Capillary circulation to the forebrain and midbrain is key to reversing memory loss, declining cognition and intelligence, dementia, and Alzheimer's disease. Therefore, the idea that Alzheimer's disease is a genetic disease has not been corroborated by verifiable science.

It is clear from the above that serotonin, acetylcholine, and dopamine mold our minds, produce our mindset or mentality, shape our good intentions and decisions, and build our character and personality. This is how neurons and neurotransmitters help us function in the community as normal, respectful, and law-abiding individuals.

Therefore, a person who cannot produce serotonin, acetylcholine, dopamine, epinephrine, and norepinephrine will have fixed ideas. Individuals who have fixed ideas are:

- Headstrong
- Obstinate
- Intransigent
- Stubborn and
- Opinionated.

If they make up their mind about something, nothing can convince them to change their mind. In other words, they cannot be persuaded to do otherwise or to reconsider their decision. Why can't they produce neurotransmitters? They cannot produce neurotransmitters because the areas where these neurotransmitters are produced are ischemic, and calcification also occurs in ischemic places.

Some young boys and girls are stubborn; they don't listen to their parents and teachers. As a result, they do what they want. Most will carry this negative attitude into adulthood and remain stubborn indefinitely. To them, changing their mind on a decision they have already made indicates weakness. No, it is not. Remaining obstinate rather betrays their mental state as a person with an ischemic brain. Their brain needed poison-less oxygenated blood since childhood, but it never received the correct blood.

Do neurotransmitters function independently of neurons? No, they don't. This question brings me to the discussion of the neuron-neurotransmitter complex.

The Neuron-Neurotransmitter Complex

Neurotransmitter	Where it is Produced
Acetylcholine	Midbrain and forebrain
Serotonin	Brain stem
Dopamine	Misbrain and hypothalamus
Epinephrine	Adrenal medulla
Norepinephrine	Adrenal medulla

The neuron/neurotransmitter complex alludes to the unceasing interdependence and interconnection between neurons and neurotransmitters. These two brain essentials are so intertwined that it is rare to see one function without the other. Interestingly, both need electricity to function.

The term "neurotransmitter" was coined from the word "neuron" to denote a chemical that transmits a message from a neuron to tissues and organs in milliseconds.

Neurotransmitters are produced in different body parts, such as the adrenal medulla, midbrain, forebrain, brain stem, hypothalamus, etc., but they are not stored where they are produced. They are stored in the neurons' axons, and there are billions of neurons. How do neurotransmitters move?

Myelin covers the axon of every neuron, and because myelin is made with lipids, it stores thermal energy. Thermal energy produces the following: forces, pressure, power, and speed. The axon harnesses pressure and power from myelin to fire a neurotransmitter across the synapse to the dendrites.

To clarify, all the 12 neurotransmitters are not stored in the axon of one neuron. How it works is that each neurotransmitter is stored in the axon of several neurons. Then, tattered myelin lacking force and power makes it impossible for the axon to fire a specific neurotransmitter to the dendrites. This explains forgetfulness, pain, trembling, lack of self-confidence, fear of heights, etc.

For example, a person cannot remember the color of a car. This shows that acetylcholine is lacking in assisting neuropeptides and neurons to remember the color of the object in question. Similarly, if a person walks into a bank, and does not remember why they came to the bank, they certainly have an acetylcholine deficiency problem.

Also, a person is in pain because endorphin, substance P, and enkephalin are not in the area where the pain is being felt. The axons that have myelin will fire these neurotransmitters, causing the pain to stop. If a person is moody, it is because their brain lacks serotonin. The axons that have myelin will fire serotonin to their brain, and the moodiness will stop. Therefore, pain, moodiness, and forgetfulness indicate the lack of a specific neurotransmitter.

A person can produce neurotransmitters, but if calculus, lithiasis, gravel, tophus, calcification, oxalates, etc., are blocking the production of myelin and the release of the neurotransmitters that were produced, the person will continue to be moody, the pain will not stop, memory loss will not stop, attention deficit disorder will not stop, and so on. Therefore, blockage is also a factor to consider.

Blockages must be removed through ionization, hydrolysis, or oxidation. If not, myelin will not be produced, and neurotransmitters and neurons won't work.

Pharmaceutical chemists don't repair myelin, their drugs don't remove blockages, and they don't help a person produce enzymes. They produce analgesics to alleviate pain, or drugs to mitigate attention deficit disorder, bipolarism, hyperactivity, etc. This is how their action causes cell neglect, resulting in constipation, moodiness, and impatience, to mention only a few side effects.

53

Quantum physics is always at work in the human body. In other words, if a specific neuron or neurotransmitter is not available to perform its function, plaque will take its place and cause the opposite of what the neuron or neurotransmitter was supposed to do. To put it simply, emptiness does not exist. Either the right protein is produced, or plaque will take its place and cause an anomaly.

Let me give the following examples to illustrate my point:

Neuron/Neurotransmitter Complex Causes	Neurofibrillary Plaque Causes
Good conduct	Bad conduct
Good behavior	Bad behavior
Good memory	Bad memory, forgetfulness
Good emotions and vibrations	Bad emotions and vibrations
Good attitude	Bad attitude
A propensity for honest behavior	A propensity for criminal behavior
A propensity for honest behavior	A propensity for dishonest behavior
Good intentions	Bad intentions
Hopefulness	Hopelessness
Encouragement	Discouragement
Self-love	Self-hatred

Love	Hatred
Empathy	Cold-heartedness
Kind-heartedness	Wickedness
Willingness to forgive	Vindictiveness
Tendency to be organized	Tendency to be messy, disorganized
Tendency to be neat	Tendency to be untidy
Tendency to be brief	Tendency to talk too much
Tendency to go straight to the point	Tendency to miss the point
Tendency to be focused	Tendency to be distracted
Tendency to address the issue	Tendency to be evasive
Tendency to be polite	Tendency to be impolite
Good Morals	Bad morals, or the lack thereof
Tendency to be considerate	Tendency to be uncaring, inconsiderate
Tendency to feel safe and secure	Tendency to feel insecure
Tendency to be consistent	Tendency to be inconsistent
Regular	Irregular
Tendency to be honest	Tendency to be dishonest, to cheat
Tendency to be honest	Tendency to be crafty or foxy

Tendency to tell the truth	Tendency to lie
The willingness to forgive	Tendency to be vindictive
Tendency to be repentant	Tendency to be remorseless
Tolerance	Intolerance
Patience	Impatience
Courage	Timidity
Boldness	Shyness
Boldness	Hesitancy
Boldness	Fearfulness, apprehension
Boldness	Nervousness
Cautiousness	Carelessness
Carefulness	Carelessness
Self-Confidence	Shyness, lack of self-confidence
Talks briefly	Loquacious, talks a lot.
Almost always on time	Almost always tardy
Calmness	Restlessness
Trustful	Paranoid, mistrustful, suspicious
Trustful	Distrustful
Trustful	Dangerous, unreliable
Calm	Agitated, on edge
Knowledgeable	Ignorant, uninformed
Willing to learn	Unwillingness to learn
Tendency to remain active	Tendency to remain inactive or passive

Affectionate	Hateful
Engaging	Cold, indifferent
Social	Anti-social
Helpful	Unhelpful
Helpful	Indifferent
Tendency to be helpful	Tendency to exploit others
Tendency to be humble	Tendency to be arrogant
Tendency to be law-abiding	Tendency to be disobedient
Tendency to be law-abiding	Tendency to break the law
Tendency to be compliant	Tendency to be non-compliant
Honest	Mischievous
Honest	Deceitful, dishonest, crafty
Tendency to be trustworthy	Tendency to be unreliable
Tendency to calm down	Tendency to become irritable
Tendency to be generous	Tendency to be thrifty, frugal
Tendency to be generous	Tendency to be selfish
Tendency to be constructive	Tendency to be destructive
Tendency to be realistic	Tendency to be unrealistic
Tendency to be realistic	Tendency to exaggerate
Tendency to be realistic	Tendency to be idealistic
Tendency to be realistic	Tendency to be unnatural

Tendency to correct mistakes	Tendency to repeat mistakes

Considering the above, any behavior or conduct that seems to be abnormal should no longer be a mystery. It is not the so-called defective genes that cause it. It is neurofibrillary plaque that is causing it.

Watch what a person does or says, and you can be a good judge of their character based on the above pointers. No matter how long it takes for a person's character flaws to become apparent, circumstances will one day expose some of their shortcomings. As a result, the decision to continue the relationship with such individuals will depend on what was observed.

However, it is a joy and a pleasure to report that there are still a few individuals in this world who are mentally and emotionally healthy enough to be trusted.

Chapter Ten

Neurotransmitters

Serotonin and dopamine are neurotransmitters mostly produced by the brain cells. The adrenal medulla produces most of the epinephrine and norepinephrine. However, none of the neurotransmitters will work if the axons of neurons cannot fire them across the synapses. The axon gets its pressure, strength, force, vigor, and power to fire neurotransmitters from myelin.

In the previous chapter, I discussed how blockages prevent the release of neurotransmitters. In this chapter, I will discuss the non-availability of myelin as the reason a person continues to be in pain, suffer memory loss, attention deficit disorder, anxiety, etc.

If the capillaries that supply oxygenated blood to myelin collapse or are occluded, the myelin cells won't divide to produce and release pressure, strength, and power to the axon to fire serotonin and dopamine across the synapse. As a result, the person will not have dopamine and serotonin. The same can also be said of the other neurotransmitters, such as:

1. Acetylcholine
2. Glutamic acid

3. Glycine
4. Y-aminobutyrate
5. Substance P
6. Enkephalin and
7. Endorphin.

There are 12 neurotransmitters, including dopamine, serotonin, epinephrine, norepinephrine, and histamine, and myelin must be available to fire them.

What does epinephrine do? Epinephrine:

1. Enhances alertness and wakefulness
2. Activates the reflexes (coughing, sneezing, running from danger, belching, hiccupping, etc.)
3. Increases the attention span and facilitates focusing and comprehension
4. Coordinates with the cardiac center in the cerebellum to monitor the heart and maintain heart function
5. Coordinates with norepinephrine, renin, ANP (atrial natriuretic peptide), and serotonin to regulate blood pressure
6. Regulates the release of histamine by the basophils, thereby controlling allergic reactions.

The adrenal medulla produces epinephrine and norepinephrine. Does the adrenal medulla have oxygenated blood? If the adrenal gland does not have oxygenated blood because the capillaries have collapsed, the person will not have epinephrine. It is the lack of epinephrine that causes:

1. Restlessness and fidgety behavior
2. Short attention span
3. Lack of self-control
4. Hyperactivity
5. Attention deficit disorder.

What does serotonin do? Serotonin:

1. Enables a person to take their mind off stressful situations so they can relax
2. Enhances calmness, thereby stopping or preventing anxiety about the present and future
3. Enhances good comprehension
4. Enhances the sense of precision
5. Enhances brevity when writing or speaking
6. Produces an eye for detail
7. Regulates a person's mood
8. Regulates a person's behavior, preventing them from breaking the law, or rules and regulations
9. Enhances digestion and metabolism
10. Regulates libido and the sex drive
11. Regulates blood pressure by making the arteries less tense
12. Creates an alternate world to reduce tension and friction
13. Enhances calmness during adversities, thereby

preventing panic attacks and anxiety

14. Eliminates fear
15. Enhances creativity to find solutions
16. Enhances self-discipline
17. Enhances self-control, thereby preventing or stopping cravings and addictions.
18. Enables a person to anticipate problems before they occur
19. Makes visionaries out of individuals
20. Enables reasoning to prevail over emotions
21. Enhances patience
22. Enhances tolerance and appreciation of diversity
23. Enhances learning from opposing views

Many neuroscientists identified the neurons that fire serotonin from the brain stem, specifically in the midline of the brain stem. Here comes the question.

Is oxygenated blood in the person's brain stem? If it is not because of capillary collapse or occlusion, the neurons will not fire serotonin, making the person:

1. Impulsive. Such individuals do not think of the consequences before they act
2. Loquacious (talk too much)
3. Suspicious
4. Nervous by nature
5. Think they are being followed

6. Weep often without cause
7. Whine or complain a lot
8. Quarrelsome
9. Tense most of the time, and a person who cannot relax will sooner or later have high blood pressure.
10. Unable to become creative enough to envisage other possibilities
11. Become fearful of failure
12. Uncertain about the future
13. Allow emotions to prevail over reasoning. Such individuals become unnecessarily emotional.

Neurons do not divide. It is the neural stem cells that divide to produce billions of neurons. After the axons of neurons have released serotonin, they fade away.

Therefore, if the neural stem cells can't divide because capillary collapse or capillary occlusion prevents them from receiving oxygenated blood, a new wave of neurons will not be produced, making it impossible for serotonin to be produced and released. Without serotonin, one or several of the following will occur:

1. Elevated blood pressure
2. Low blood pressure
3. Tense arteries
4. Apprehension
5. Depression

6. Suicidal tendencies
7. Inability to cope with stress
8. Fear of heights
9. Fear of dogs
10. Fear of snakes or crawlers
11. Fear of approaching corners
12. Fear of ghosts or haunted places
13. Fear of thunderstorms
14. A general feeling of insecurity
15. Fear of being on the ocean
16. Unnecessary worries
17. Wild and baseless imaginations causing more apprehension
18. Entertaining crazy ideas.

Also, the absence of serotonin causes the following bad habits:

1. Lack of self-control (alcoholism, addiction to painkillers, vaping, or sex; addiction to indigestible items such as chalk, paper, crayons, pencil, clay, ice chewing, etc; addiction to sugar, salt, fruits, tomatoes, potatoes, or nuts, etc.; addiction to illegal drugs such as cocaine, methamphetamine, LSD (Lysergic Acid Diethylamide), and addiction to attention (wants to be seen and heard).
2. Lack of self-discipline
3. Bullying

4. Tendency to pick on the weak and defenseless
5. Sadism or the tendency to hurt others for the fun of it
6. Tendency to make light of a person's tragedy
7. Tendency to make fun of how people talk, walk, etc.
8. Tendency to laugh at a person who slips and falls
9. Tendency to repeat over and over what they heard
10. General repetitive behavior
11. A habit of not listening when others are talking
12. A habit of not allowing others to complete their sentences
13. Domineering attitude
14. Tendency to present oneself as healthy despite illness or the habit of living under pretenses.

Countless individuals who are depressed take pills because they are told they lack serotonin. What will pills do? Can they reverse ischemia (bloodlessness) in the brain stem? No, they cannot. A person becomes suicidal because their brain stem cannot produce serotonin. Counseling them will not help because counseling does not restore capillary circulation to the brain stem.

Meditation was invented to help people relax and cope with stress. A person does not need meditation to relax. Serotonin is the neurotransmitter that enables a person to relax naturally and overcome stress by creating new possibilities.

Therefore, instead of focusing on meditation, people should focus on revitalizing their collapsed cerebral capillaries, or they can do both, meaning do meditation and also revitalize the collapsed capillaries that have made their brain stem ischemic.

Chapter Eleven

The Health and Role of Neurons and Neurotransmitters

What do neurons do so they are not confused with the nerves? Most neurons assist the nerves and neurotransmitters in making them extremely efficient.

Neurons are responsible for good behavior, conduct, and mobility (walking in a straight line, jogging, running, dancing, etc.). Then, they team up with neurotransmitters to make us function like normal individuals in the community.

A few neurons connect with other neurons to produce ideas. Without these ideas, concepts, and principles the world would not have been built and transformed. Therefore, we owe creation to neurons. Also, neurons enabled me to invent Symptometry and Symptometric science in sharp contrast to medical science. Then, there are neurons in the brain stem that produce serotonin.

A neuron is not like the average body cell. Its plasma membrane is different because it has a leakage channel, which other cells and stem cells do not have. It is because neurons are built for speed and last for only a few minutes that what nourishes them is not the same as what nourishes the bone cells and other cells.

A neuron's ability to function depends on its inside concentration of potassium and outside concentration of sodium. If a person does not eat salt for sodium, their outside sodium concentration will be too low, affecting their neurons' electrical activity.

As copper provides the neurons with speed, the leakage channel in the neuron's plasma membrane allows sodium to get into the neuron and potassium to get out of the neuron at top speed several times a minute. This is how neurons produce electricity for themselves. Then, they get speed from copper.

Does the person eat the food sources of copper, and after eating these foods, are they able to digest copper? After digesting copper, is copper in their bloodstream? If copper, sodium, potassium, and iron are not in their bloodstream, their neuronal connections will be too slow, causing the following:

1. Weak memory.
2. Slow in thinking and processing thoughts.
3. Slow in doing basic arithmetic.
4. Slow comprehension. The person must read the paragraph a few times to understand part of the

message, or the question must be repeated.

5. The person walks, talks, drives slowly, etc. Also, the person cannot decide on the spur of the moment. They must take days to decide.

6. Slow or diminished reflexes.

Autism is fundamentally a neuronal connectivity problem. The absence of conductors of electricity from the blood causes a few cases of autism, while the non-production of neurons, neurotransmitters, and enzymes causes the remaining instances of autism.

Vaccination causing autism is coincidental. Every child that is vaccinated does not become autistic. I was vaccinated. I am not autistic.

It is a fact that there is thimerosal (mercury) in vaccines, and mercury is poison. Then, there is sorbitol and other adjuvants in vaccines. If certain acidic fruits are eaten on the day the child is vaccinated, their chances of developing poor neuronal connections become extremely high.

Some children have neuronal connectivity problems, but they are not autistic. They are intellectually slow, but not autistic. For instance, countless students are intellectually slow.

The fact is that the activities of neurons and neurotransmitters make a person intellectually smart, mentally and emotionally stable, and healthy. Then, it is the following factors that determine whether a person is mentally healthy and stable or not:

1. Nutrients that are needed but cannot get into the bloodstream.
2. Availability or non-availability of oxygenated blood.
3. Cell nourishment or neurofibrillary plaque.
4. Enzyme production or non-production of enzymes and
5. Production or non-production of neurons and neurotransmitters.

Conduct an observational experiment by sitting 300 individuals in an auditorium to listen to a 30-minute lecture. How many individuals out of these 300 will have a good attention span lasting for 30 minutes and a good memory to remember the highlights of the lecture 30 minutes later? The number will be fewer than eight. The same can be said of a congregation that listens to a bishop's Sunday sermon.

People cannot pay attention, and have a good memory and intellect if they cannot produce neurons, enzymes, or neurotransmitters, and they eat chaotically. Additionally, the midbrain of most of these individuals is ischemic.

How many college students have a good memory? The answer is, very few, and the saddest part of this statistic is that they do not know what it takes to have an excellent memory and good learning skills. How many students are in the top 5 in their class? The answer is very few. The rest have problems expressing their thoughts, memorizing lessons, understanding lessons, etc., but they will pass because the passing grades in many colleges and universities are low.

The best advice for having an excellent memory is to have poison-less oxygenated blood in the hippocampus around the clock. The emphasis is on the adjective "poison-less" because poison denatures and deactivates enzymes, and nothing will be produced without enzymes.

A good memory goes hand-in-hand with the ability to acquire new skills, and a good learning skill is required to facilitate learning. How? By reorganizing the lecture. Reorganization requires highlighting or summarizing the key ideas in the lecture and citing examples to support them. It is the student's input that enhances learning.

For example, the facts about neurotransmitters are scattered throughout this lecture. Condense them and bring only the key neurotransmitters, where they are produced, and what they do into a sharp focus on flashcards. Then, memorize what you wrote. This is why I said, "A good memory goes hand-in-hand with acquiring new skills" and learning requires reorganizing facts.

What does dopamine do?

Dopamine:

1. Emboldens a person to the point where they become fearless of consequences.
2. Makes a person defy the odds.
3. Stabilizes the nerves.
4. Enhances movement. In other words, it is the neurotransmitter for mobility. Therefore, a person who keeps depleting dopamine will increase his or her chances of becoming paralyzed.
5. Enhances coordination during movement, allowing a person to walk straight while thinking, processing thoughts, and activating memory.
6. Enhances risk-taking.
7. Stimulates the drive for adventurism, exploration, etc.
8. Makes a person fearless of the unknown, wanting to try something new, test a new idea, etc.
9. Enables a person to anticipate consequences before taking any action.
10. Motivates a person to travel. It enables a person who lost their home to start all over, start a new project or a new business, engage in research and discoveries, etc.
11. Fills a person with hope. It fills them with the determination and zeal to learn, succeed, etc.

12. Makes a person turn failure into lessons to learn.

13. Makes a person never give up. Hence, the expression "Where there is a will, there is a way."

14. Makes a person a fearless competitor.

15. Brightens the future.

16. Enables a person to explore new ideas.

17. Gives a person a sense of purpose, pleasure, content, and happiness or something to be happy about.

18. Makes a person bring out the best in others.

19. Enhances concentration or focus.

20. Elevates a person's mood.

21. Assists acetylcholine in enhancing learning and acquiring a new skill.

22. Enables a person to consider a loss as an opportunity to rebuild better.

23. Enhances self-satisfaction or makes a person know their limit.

Several parts of the brain produce dopamine, but most of the dopamine is made in the substantia nigra, ventral tegmental area, and hypothalamus. Here are the questions. *Is poison-less oxygenated blood in the parts of the brain where dopamine is produced? Is the enzyme called dopamine hydroxylase available to convert norepinephrine to dopamine?* If this enzyme is not available, and the parts that produce dopamine are ischemic, dopamine will not be produced, causing the person to become:

1. Fearful
2. Afraid of the unknown
3. Afraid of traveling by plane
4. Afraid of traveling by boat
5. Devoid of a sense of purpose
6. Devoid of a sense of humor
7. Panicky
8. Nailbiter
9. Hair puller
10. Lip chewer
11. Teeth grinder
12. Devoid of self-confidence
13. Devoid of self-determination
14. Overcome by anxiety
15. Intensely suspicious
16. Unnecessarily aggressive
17. Extremely edgy and insecure
18. Dismissive of adventures and explorations
19. Hesitant to try something new
20. Hesitant to buy new items
21. Hesitant to move to a better place
22. Slow to adapt to a new environment
23. Hesitant to take risks.

Dopamine is the only neurotransmitter that is produced by conversion. Its absence causes the following bad habits:

1. Bruxism (teeth grinding)

2. Thumbsucking or finger sucking
3. Cloth chewing
4. Nail biting
5. Lip chewing
6. Lip twisting
7. Nose digging or picking
8. Self-abuse with a sharp object
9. Bedwetting
10. Talking in sleep
11. Fast eating
12. Hair pulling
13. Hair twirling
14. Lying or finding it difficult to tell the truth
15. Stealing
16. Running away from home
17. Not sleeping enough
18. Humming
19. Whistling
20. Masturbating
21. Head banging
22. Nibbling (snacking all day)
23. Binge eating
24. People pleasing
25. Procrastinating
26. Staying up late
27. Exercising excessively or addiction to exercise
28. Repeating a question before answering it
29. Fidgeting

What does acetylcholine do?

Acetylcholine:

1. Ends sleep and wakes us up. In other words, it ends the effect of melatonin on the brain.
2. Prevents or ends coma by countering the effect of melatonin on the central nervous system.
3. Builds and maintains memory. A good memory enables a person to remember names, addresses, places, phone numbers, faces, descriptions, lessons, sizes of items, and the colors of objects.
4. Facilitates fast recall.
5. Enhances the desire and willingness to correct mistakes.
6. Facilitates and enhances learning and stimulates the desire to know more by asking questions.
7. Enables a person to pay attention and focus on a task or activity.
8. Enhances alertness.
9. Enhances cognition.
10. Enhances balance when walking in a straight line.
11. Enhances understanding or comprehension.
12. Enhances clarity of thought and expression when talking or writing.
13. Enhances simplicity of expression, the use of the right words in the right context, and coherence when speaking or writing.

14. Makes a person conscious of their environment.
15. Makes a person remember landmarks to retrace their footsteps.
16. Enhances character judgment.

Acetylcholine is produced by the cells in the mid-brain and forebrain, specifically in the nucleus of Meyner and the medial septal nucleus, and for it to be made, there must be poison-less oxygenated blood in the mid-brain and forebrain at all times.

If the forebrain and midbrain are calcified because the capillaries that supply oxygenated blood to it collapsed or became occluded and have not been revitalized, it will be impossible to produce acetylcholine. This explains why people suffer from brain fog, memory loss, amnesia, dementia, or Alzheimer's disease. Let me take a moment to discuss neurofibrillary plaque and its dark side.

Chapter Twelve
The Dark Side of
Neurofibrillary Plaque

Neurofibrillary plaque gets a person stuck in one bad habit, conduct, behavior, etc., or with one opinion, prejudice, intention, etc. As a result, they cannot change their habit, behavior, or conduct, no matter how hard they try. This is why a thief will always be a thief; a murderer will always be a murderer, a cheat will always be a cheat, a child molester will always be a child molester, etc. Counseling is a waste of time because it won't work on such individuals.

It is neurofibrillary plaque that brings out the worst in a person and makes some of us descend into the abyss of bestiality, where we behave like animals.

Animals are predators; they only take care of themselves and their cubs; they don't care for the weak, and their only intention is to survive, even if it is at the expense of other animals. To them, survival requires killing another animal.

Also, animals are territorial, and they don't share what they have with other animals. Don't many of us exhibit these tendencies? Yes, many do.

The Underlying Causes of Mental Anomalies

Getting a master's degree or a doctorate or being a professional does not make us better individuals. Also, being a religious devotee does not make us better individuals. It is the amount of plaque or oxygenated blood in our cerebral cortex that determines our personality.

I have often heard the expression, "We are not perfect" The question is, have people taken their time to know *why* we are not "perfect"? No, they have not. Imperfection and mediocrity are our own making. We can always do better and become better individuals if we take care of our brains.

Have humans changed since this world was created? No. We are still the same with the same character flaws regardless of our age, tribe, culture, gender, socio-economic status, and skin color. The landscape and the skyline keep changing. There are more places of convenience, means of transportation, and amenities abound, but, on the whole, the flaws in humans are still the same.

The difference Symptometry is trying to make is to bring these character flaws to people's attention and expose their sources. Probably, by letting people know the source of their character flaws (capillary collapse and occlusion, and neurofibrillary plaque), some of them will call Symptometry to help them reverse these character flaws.

The tendency to steal and lie is in many primary school children. Therefore, for parents to assume that their children will grow out of mischief, lying, or stealing is an illusion. These negative tendencies must be brought to Symptometry's attention so they are nipped in the bud as quickly as possible. It is only when they are nipped in the bud that character flaws will stop ruining the child's personality. How are they nipped in the bud? It is done by ionizing neurofibrillary plaque that blocks circulation to the forebrain, midbrain, and brain stem, and by committing to scientific cooking, eating, and living.

I must admit that many individuals grew to become honest, truthful, and trustworthy without Symptometry. How did they do it? What happened was, even though their other body parts were ischemic, they had enough blood to produce neurons and neurotransmitters in their midbrain, brain stem, hypothalamus, and forebrain. This was how they produced neurons and serotonin for good behavior and conduct.

Symptometry is still available to those who do not have oxygenated blood in their forebrains, midbrains, and brain stems.

It is stated in the anatomy books that the cerebral cortex molds or shapes a person's personality, but these books never explain how personality is molded and what molds it. It turns out that it is the neurons and neurotransmitters that team up to mold a person's personality in the cerebral cortex.

Unfortunately, if the capillaries that supply poison-less

oxygenated blood to the cerebral cortex collapse, or are occluded, ischemia will occur in the cerebral cortex, and the formation of neurofibrillary plaque will follow ischemia.

Therefore, a person's attitude, likes, dislikes, preferences, temperament, reactions, behavior, or conduct speaks volumes about what is happening to their brain.

Even though I devoted a lot of time to the discussion of neurotransmitters and neurons, the stem cells that produce neurons use enzymes to divide, clean themselves, clear the pathways, neutralize poisons, protect themselves from harm, and nourish themselves.

Then, the neurons must have myelin. How do the neural stem cells produce myelin for the neurons? They use the enzymes called polymerases.

Chapter Thirteen

Enzymes and

Neurotransmitters

As I mentioned earlier, it is poison-less oxygenated blood full of nutrients and resources that enables the cells to use nutrients to produce enzymes.

Enzymes are our cells' work tools in the same manner that a mechanic, electrician, plumber, and carpenter have their work tools. However, unlike carpenters, plumbers, etc., who buy their work tools, human cells make their work tools to help them achieve all their objectives. These work tools are called enzymes.

The enzymes called permeases feed the cells by modifying the nutrients' structures so they can penetrate each brain cell, measuring between 28 and 32 microns.

Isomerases rearrange the nutrients on the enzyme template so acetylcholine, dopamine, norepinephrine, etc., can be produced according to the blueprint's specifications. The enzyme called myelin polymerase speeds up the production of myelin, so the axons of neurons have myelin.

Then, 19 digestive enzymes extract nutrients from the

food they digest. The question is, why aren't there enough nutrients in the blood to produce enzymes? I will explain.

Heavy metals are in the food people eat, and at the point of assimilation in the small intestine, the minerals with heavier atomic weight eliminate the minerals with light atomic weight, thereby denying the minerals with light-atomic weight like calcium, magnesium, copper, chromium, iron, cobalt, manganese, etc. entry into the bloodstream. It is the blockage of entry into the bloodstream that causes nutrient deficiencies. I will elaborate on this fact of life by citing a few examples.

- Bismuth in wheat, barley, and sorghum has an atomic weight of 209.
- Cadmium in wheat, teff, and barley has an atomic weight of 113.
- Lead in unsafe drinking water has an atomic weight of 207.
- Mercury in vaccines, certain fish, and dental fillings has an atomic weight of 201.
- Molybdenum in certain dietary supplements and prenatal supplements has an atomic weight of 96.

Because these minerals are heavier than the light-atomic weight nutrients, they make it impossible for the following mineral nutrients, amino acids, and vitamins to get into the bloodstream:

- Calcium with an atomic weight of 40
- Copper with an atomic weight of 63
- Chromium with an atomic weight of 51
- Cobalt with an atomic weight of 59
- Iron with an atomic weight of 56
- Magnesium with an atomic weight of 24
- Manganese with an atomic weight of 55
- Oxygen with an atomic weight of 16
- Potassium with an atomic weight of 19
- Selenium with an atomic weight of 79 and
- Zinc with an atomic weight of 65.

Amino acids and vitamins have no atomic weight, and if they cannot get into the bloodstream, how can the cells use them to produce enzymes? They can't.

If iron, zinc, and manganese cannot be in the bloodstream to activate the enzymes that the cells just produced, enzymes will not be activated to speed up the production of neurotransmitters. As a result, the person won't have dopamine, serotonin, epinephrine, etc. This explains a person's inability to produce neurotransmitters.

Since wheat is eaten all over the world, what does Symptometry recommend that wheat eaters do so they can get vitamins, amino acids, and light minerals into their brain cells? It recommends scientific eating.

Scientific eating is a way of life. It enables a health-conscious person to avoid foods made from wheat for a day or two. During the abstinence from wheat they are advised to produce a lot of GTH transferase to neutralize the heavy metal ions in their system.

After the heavy minerals have been neutralized, amino acids, vitamins, and light-weight minerals can move into the bloodstream; and the cells can use them to produce countless enzymes. This is as far as getting nutrients into the bloodstream is concerned.

Two other concerns that must be addressed are enzyme denaturing and enzyme deactivation. Individuals cannot produce neurotransmitters because they denature their enzymes, deactivate them, and cannot produce enzyme activators.

What denatures enzymes? The following items denature enzymes

Alcohol. Our liver produces an enzyme called alcohol dehydratase to detoxify alcohol. Therefore, a person who does not know what it takes to produce alcohol dehydratase and drinks alcohol will surely denature all the enzymes that are used to produce acetylcholine for memory, serotonin, and dopamine. Then, they will produce alcohol receptors in the pleasure center within their hippocampus. It is these receptors that will cause alcohol addiction in addition to mental aberrations.

Toxic Metals. Mercury, arsenic, lead, etc., denature digestive enzymes as well as the enzymes that accelerate the production of acetylcholine. If a person's liver can produce the enzyme called alcohol dehydratase, these toxic metals will be neutralized, but if their liver cannot produce it, or it produces it and is denatured, these toxic metals will never allow neurotransmitters to work in their body. As a result, their mental aberration will become chronic

Pharmaceutical Drugs. All pharmaceutical drugs have alkyl. The liver produces the enzyme called GTH transferase to detoxify pharmaceutical drugs, but if the person's liver cannot produce GTH transferase and they take pharmaceutical drugs, they won't be able to produce acetylcholine, dopamine, epinephrine, serotonin, and other neurotransmitters. Also, alkyl eliminates hydrogen, and without hydrogen, albumins cannot cause osmosis. It is osmosis that makes water available to the cells. Without water, our cells cannot function.

Radioactive Isotopes And Radiation. Iodine 123, 125, and 131, which are used in hospitals for screening certain diseases, are radioactive isotopes. The liver produces the enzyme called radioisotope transferase to neutralize radioactive isotopes so they do not denature enzymes. Still if the person's liver cannot produce radioisotope transferase, radioactive isotopes will accumulate in them, denaturing the enzymes that accelerate the production of acetylcholine, serotonin, norepinephrine, epinephrine, and dopamine. Such widespread denaturing will make the person dysfunctional because they cannot produce neurotransmitters.

Acidosis. Acids denature enzymes.

Alkalosis. Alkalis denature enzymes.

Enzymes that are denatured and enzymes that poisons deactivate are worthless. Poisons are found in:

The food most of us eat. Look for the list of poisons from the American School of Symptometry, NFP, to know where to find them.

The industrial chemicals to which some of us expose ourselves, especially in our workplaces, deactivate our enzymes.

People wonder why they suddenly become mentally incompetent or imbalanced, why they start hearing voices, seeing what the average person does not see, etc. Why do they smell what people around them do not smell, etc.? Then, they start entertaining weird thoughts, motives, etc. What happened?

What happened was that they have not been producing

neurotransmitters, and this has been going on for at least a decade, and now, enzyme denaturing and deactivation have caught up to them. They can go on blaming cocaine, marijuana, methamphetamine, alcohol, etc., for causing these mental aberrations, but the hard truth is that they have never produced many neurotransmitters in decades.

The idea that some individuals see demons when they close their eyes or that evil spirits, etc., possess them could make it impossible for them to reverse ischemia and neurofibrillary plaque. Why? The answer is their mind is already messed up.

The brain is where good decisions are made with neurotransmitters, or bad decisions are made without neurotransmitters.

Parents and loved ones can persuade a mentally ill person to stick to the Symptometry recovery plan, but is the person ready to recover from their mental aberration? If they are not ready because they cannot produce neurotransmitters, then the parents who are persuading them to do Symptometry are wasting their time. After all is said and done, the final decision rests with the sick person, not with the parents.

Diagnosing mental aberrations by calling them schizophrenia, multiple personality disorder, bipolar disorder, neurosis, psychosis, etc., totally misses the point.

Then, treating these mental aberrations, such as narcissism, sociopathy, and psychopathy, with psychiatric drugs makes matters worse. Have pharmaceutical drugs ever reversed a person's mental illness? Never, and I just explained why. They cannot because they have alkyl and halogen.

Also, without oxygenated blood in the midbrain, brain stem, forebrain, neurons, and enzymes, neurotransmitters will not be produced. Therefore, if neurotransmitters cannot be produced and neural stem cells cannot divide to produce neurons – game over.

In narcissism, the person is so self-centered that they love only themselves and care only for themselves. A sociopath impulsively disregards the rights and feelings of others and has no concept of right and wrong. A psychopath is manipulative, deceitful, shameless, callous, and remorseless.

Narcissism, sociopathy, neurosis, psychosis, and psychopathy started in childhood, and the situation that was left unattended became worse over the years. Can a person who has these personality disorders be redeemed? It depends on them.

Can they take the initiative to call Symptometry for assistance? It is up to them. Some individuals are so far gone that their personality cannot be normalized. Such individuals commit suicide. Others allow diseases to kill them because they no longer have the will to live. In Symptometry, a person who does not request assistance should be left alone.

Activation of Enzymes

An enzyme can be produced, but it will not work unless it is activated. The six enzyme activators are:

1. Iron
2. Zinc
3. Copper
4. Manganese
5. ATP and
6. Decarboxylase.

Carpenters have work tools, and so do plumbers, mechanics, electricians, pipefitters, trench diggers, commodity traders, surgeons, diagnosticians, journalists, dentists, lumberjacks, tailors, etc. Our cells are also workers. Unlike professionals who buy their work tools, our cells produce their work tools, and their work tools are called enzymes. Enzymes come already packed with electrical energy.

Enzyme Energy

Where do enzymes get their energy from? The three resources that enzymes use to break bonds and facilitate circulation are magnetic energy, electrical energy, and thermal energy.

It is the magnetic energy from human infrared radiation that pulls the ions (atoms) of nutrients to the template. Isomerases use electrical energy to rearrange the nutrient ions on the enzyme template, placing amino acids, base triplets, and cofactors where they should be. Welding is done with thermal energy to secure the template.

Heat from mitochondrial energy, hot peppers, and hot water provide enzymes with thermal energy. Electricity to make enzymes work faster comes from the following sources: 1) electrolytes, 2) cations from good salt, 3) electricity from mitochondrial energy, 4) the conductors of electricity, and 5) water. Then, enzymes tap magnetism from the brain and the body's magnetic field.

BSE (basic support energy), aka sustainable energy, provides the template with enzymatic energy, also known as operational energy. After the enzyme has been activated, it latches into the substrate so operational energy can spin both.

Modus Operandi

Many other enzymes do not spin the substrate. They work directly on the substrate, breaking its bonds, chipping away the bonds piece by piece, adding water to the bonds, etc., until the substrate disintegrates.

Since our cells produce enzymes to divide them, unwind DNA, repair themselves, nourish themselves, repair DNA and ribosomal RNA, produce mitochondrial energy, protect themselves from harm, protect their products from harm, clean themselves, clean the blood and the lymphatic system, and pick apart poisons, acids, alkaloids, toxic acids, metabolites, concretions, and hindrances to ease circulation, they will cause anomalies only if they have not received nutrients and resources in weeks, or something happens to their work tools or DNA.

What could happen to their work tools?

- Enzymes could be denatured or deactivated, making them worthless. Acidosis, alkalosis, excessive radiation, radioactive isotopes, pharmaceutical drugs, and toxic metals denature enzymes, and poisons deactivate enzymes. Unless the poison is neutralized by allosteric poison binders, the replacement enzyme that ribosomal RNA produces will not last. Does the person know how to help their ribosomal RNA produce allosteric poison binders?

What could happen to DNA?

- A phosphoprotein could hydroxylate (damage) tyrosine, threonine, or serine, making it impossible to transmit the base triplets or codons of tyrosine, threonine, and serine to ribosomal RNA. A hormone, neurotransmitter, or protein cannot be produced without the base triplets. Also, destroying three amino acids leaves only 17 amino acids in DNA. Since 17 amino acids are not the full set of purines and pyrimidines, DNA will be so weak that it will fall apart, causing fragmentation. This is how the phosphoproteins a person eats without producing enzymes to protect the amino acids in DNA can cause susceptibility to anomalies.

Carcinogens could eliminate cysteine from DNA and block its reintegration into DNA, causing a mutation. This is how cancer occurs in a person. Homocysteine, a metabolite of methionine, is one of the major concerns of the cardiovascular system. Of all the crops that humans consume, rice has the largest amount of methionine, and it is because it also has arsenic and a lot of starch that it produces the toughest homocysteine. Without the enzyme called homocysteine reductase, homocysteine will not disintegrate.

Cumulative homocysteine is produced when a person eats rice, beans, eggs, cheese, fish, or meat in 24 hours and does not produce homocysteine reductase to remove homocysteine.

Homocysteine is known to cause stenosis or even ischemia. It is also known for making the arteries tense and interfering with the sodium/potassium pump, making it one of the worst blood pressure deregulators of our time. Additionally, it may cause chest pain and muscle tightness in the chest or calves.

Hence, there is a connection between what a person eats and their anomalies, especially if they cannot produce enzymes or they produce the enzyme but cannot activate it.

There are enzymes to digest starch and enzymes to digest methionine. While amylase digests starch, homocysteine reductase must break down methionine and liberate its sulfur. If methionine is not broken down, homocysteine may start damaging some cells.

There is so much clutter, filth, or garbage in the blood that leaving blood in such a state would only slow down blood traffic and cause enzyme denaturation, deactivation, and mayhem. Therefore, if a person cannot produce the above-mentioned path clearers to clear the way to facilitate the fast circulation of nutrients, resources, hormones, neurotransmitters, peptides, etc., the cells won't get any assistance to self-correct and produce what needs to be produced.

Our cells can do everything to make us healthy, but we must provide them with what they need, in the right amount and at the right time, and follow the rules that govern our existence on this planet.

The Underlying Causes of Mental Anomalies

Blood is naturally dirty, and if enzymes are not produced to clean it every day, anomalies will not be reversed. For instance, hydrogen cyanide, methane, and hydrogen sulfide will weaken immunity so badly that the body can no longer beat back microbial attacks.

Infections or inflammation will occur in the gums, teeth, bladder, stomach, skin, ears, etc., and this is because the unremoved filth in the blood has turned into microbial growth factors.

Herbalists use what they call alteratives (blood purifiers) to make their clients believe that their blood is being sanitized. How can herbs or bark of trees cleanse a person's blood?

There are toxic gases, concretions, poisons, alkaloids, recombinants, oxalates, fat globules, etc., in the blood. What is the herb removing? What are the acupuncture needles removing? What is a chiropractor removing when they are adjusting a person's spine, neck, etc.? These remain open questions.

What about physicians? What do pharmaceutical drugs remove from a person's dirty blood? They do not remove anything. They would rather add more garbage to the existing pile of garbage.

People have never questioned the quality of their blood,

and no blood test can help a physician determine how dirty or clean a person's blood is. Blood is dirty, and it is only enzymes that can clean a person's blood.

Do these enzymes come from dietary supplements? Yes, some of them do, but the supplements must be properly combined.

However, most enzymes come from subatomic particles. Why? The answer is that they are not inert like pharmaceutical drugs, herbs, and many dietary supplements, and they are not as weak as the nutrients in the food we eat. They are loaded with magnetic energy, thermal energy, and electrical energy, as well as power, force, pressure, and strength thanks to succussion. This is the difference.

Acupuncture, chiropractic, allopathic medicine, and herbalists, as well as Chinese medical practitioners, have never talked about enzymes because enzymes do not apply to what they do. If they do not apply to what they do, how can the cells of the people they treat divide, self-correct, and self-regulate?

They all focus on treatment products and procedures. Never on cleaning the blood and attending to the well-being of the cells, DNA, and chromosomes, and never on the production of enzymes, their activation, and preservation. Therefore, what we in Symptometry do is not what they do.

Description of Enzymes

Our cells produce over 64 different types of enzymes. They produce some enzymes in the hundreds and dozens of others. Most enzymes are holoenzymes.

Composition of Enzymes

Most enzymes are holoenzymes, meaning they are made of amino acids (protein), vitamins, and minerals. Protein, aka amino acids, forms the apoenzyme. Vitamins are the cofactors.

Therefore, a holoenzyme consists of an apoenzyme and a cofactor. The genetic code is in the protein or amino acid (the apoenzyme).

However, silicon is the only mineral that produces enzymes by itself. It pulls amino acids, minerals, or vitamins to make enzymes and also activates them. No wonder this is the mineral that plants use to produce their enzymes. Does this mean that we can use plant enzymes because they are mostly made with silicon? No. Plants use silicon to produce their enzymes. We must also use silicon to produce our enzymes. Plants are not humans.

Function of Enzymes

Enzymes play a significant role in cell division, cell

97

protection, cell repair, circulation, and the production of hormones, neurotransmitters, desmosomes, polypeptides, etc. How? By repairing DNA. Every production in the human body starts with helicase unwinding DNA. However, if DNA is fragmented, it must be repaired.

It is after DNA polymerase has repaired DNA that the gene/DNA alignment can be restored, and the alignment between DNA and the three RNAs can also be restored.

Then, after the double alignment has been restored, the gene can release the blueprint to DNA for onward transmission to messenger RNA, transfer RNA, and ribosomal RNA. In other words, if DNA is not repaired, hormones, neurotransmitters, etc. will not be produced.

Some enzymes are multipurpose chemicals. A few are single-purpose enzymes. The speed at which ribosomal RNA produces enzymes or proteins depends on whether it is an emergency or not.

For example, ribosomal RNA will produce enzymes faster and by the thousands if a person's life is in danger, such as poisoning. Under such circumstances, allosteric poison binders, allosteric chemical binders, hydratases, and transferases will be produced by the thousands and in several rounds, provided the person is not fed in a day or two. In other words, not eating is helpful to cell repair. This may explain why the sick person who wants to recover does not have an appetite for food and refuses to eat.

If a person is starving, their cells will immediately change their tactics. They will resort to rationing nutrients and water, and to achieve this objective, they will produce rationing enzymes. Such enzymes will ration and stretch the nutrients and resources as far as they can. Then, they will shut down the three energy zappers, which are the brain and the nervous system, the muscular system, and the digestive system.

After four days without food and water, the cells' emergency procedures will make the starving person extremely weak, frail, and thin. Some individuals have survived for one week without food and water, causing their cells to change tactics again.

After spending five to seven days without food and water, the cells turn to stored fat and protein for energy and nourishment. This will go on until the person is found and rescued. If not, the body will turn into a cesspool of poisons. Finally, internal poisons will deactivate oxidase and terminate the person's life.

Energy Requirement for Enzymes

Basic support energy is the product of total mitochondrial energy produced minus the physical, mental, and digestive energy used. The three major users of mitochondrial energy are the brain and nervous system, the muscular system, and the digestive system.

Then, the ratio of the energy used to the amount of energy saved depends on the person's profession or vocation. For example, a sedentary person who does mental and intellectual work more than physical work will use about 60% of their BSE doing mental work.

Conversely, a person whose vocation or profession requires physical labor must eat heavier meals and use more muscle power and strength to work. Such a person will spend about 80% of their BSE doing physical work and digesting food while using the remaining 20% of BSE doing mental work, sleeping, eliminating waste, breathing, etc. How much BSE will be left to activate enzymes? Nothing. Enzymes are not activated with deficits. Zinc, iron, copper, etc., activate enzymes with BSE surpluses.

We must plan our daily routines and eat foods that leave us with at least 10% of BSE, which is enough to activate all the enzymes in our body for one day.

If enzymes are not activated, they won't work. Also, if enzymes are denatured or deactivated, they won't work. A person in whom enzymes do not work won't be healthy in many parts of their body. After all is said and done, health begins with the enzyme called helicase, and life begins and ends with the enzyme called oxidase.

Unless the enzyme called helicase unwinds DNA so that DNA can unzip to expose the genes that are on the chromosomes, the transmission of the codon to messenger RNA will never happen. This is what is meant by "health begins with helicase."

Those who do not know about enzymes should know about them now before it is too late. They are indispensable to cellular activities, and they are terrific. Call them the little geniuses of Wonderland, and you will never be wrong. They are superfast, on point, on time, precise, and exceed all expectations.

Enzymes pick apart toxic gases and poisons to make them harmless and remove the hindrances that are on and inside the cells, nuclei, cytoplasm, cytosol, tissues, organs, and membranes. They also remove hindrances in venous blood, arterial blood, and lymphatic vessels to facilitate fast circulation and the production of essentials. Such cleansing allows a strong heart to keep pumping cleaner blood to circulate essentials for decades.

Also, enzymes build, rebuild, and fortify the cells, ligaments, tendons, cartilage, viscus (an internal organ), valves, sphincters, sinuses, tissues, blood vessels, and lymphatic vessels.

During gestation, enzymes build every body part under the supervision of the trophoblast. Shortly before birth, enzymes make the trophoblast disappear.

Nineteen (19) digestive enzymes enable nutrients to get into the bloodstream, allowing the ancillary enzymes to take over, cleaning the blood, nourishing the cells, rebuilding and fortifying the blood vessels, lymphatic vessels, etc. Cell nourishment results in the production of essentials by ribosomal RNA.

Why does a person who is mentally ill suffer from memory loss, declining cognition, etc.? The answer is their midbrain is so ischemic that they cannot produce acetylcholine, neurons, and enzymes due to capillary collapse and occlusion.

Chapter Fourteen
A Closer Look At A Diagnosis

A diagnosis is an allopathic process of naming a disease after studying reported or observed symptoms. A prescription or surgery almost always follows a diagnosis.

A prescription is based on the recommendations of the book called PDR (physicians' desk reference). As standard procedure, this book provides a wide variety of pharmaceutical drugs that can be prescribed for each diagnosis.

I am familiar with the medical system because I was born into it, just like billions of others. I was vaccinated and treated for fever, malaria, influenza, you name it. Now that I am a senior citizen on Medicare, I am back into it, but this time with a difference. The difference is that I submit to the various clinical tests, and if there are red flags in these tests, I know what to do. I do not take pharmaceuticals unless for emergency purposes.

Here is what should be known about a medical diagnosis, and this extends to the psychiatric diagnosis.

A diagnosis facilitates allopathic treatment, but it never addresses the source of the disease. What is the source of every disease? The answer is dirty blood, meaning blood full of impurities including poisons and toxins.

How did the person get this kind of blood? They got it from eating foods for which they were not producing enzymes to break down poisons and toxins, as well as blood clots, concretions, sludge, and debris. As a result, all these impurities remained in the blood.

Also, capillary collapse and occlusion cause widespread ischemia. Ischemia causes atrophies, or the formation of plaque and calcifications in the brain, organs, membranes, cartilage, tendons, etc. This is the logical sequence of events calling for cell-based Symptometry.

The diagnosis can still stand as ADD, ADHD, bipolar disorder, schizophrenia, neurosis, psychosis, sociopathy, psychopathy, personality disorder, dementia, amnesia, Alzheimer's disease, etc., but if the person prefers Symptometry or their parents prefer Symptometry to psychiatric treatment, they will increase their chances of benefitting from cell self-correction, self-protection, self-nourishment, self-cleansing, and self-perpetuation.

Cell self-correction, self-nourishment, etc., will never take place unless the person is committed to the scientific selection of foods, scientific cooking, scientific eating, and scientific living.

The Underlying Causes of Mental Anomalies

The scientific selection of foods to cook stops filling the person's blood with poisons, thereby reducing the poison load and increasing their chances for recovery. Symptometry's particulates and molecules enable the person's cells to produce the following enzymes:

1. Path cleaners to facilitate the transport of nutrients and ionize debris and blood clots.
2. Allosteric poison busters to neutralize poisons from lettuce, nuts, potato, tomato, etc.
3. Allosteric chemical busters.
4. Constitutive enzymes.
5. Phospholipase to repair the plasma membrane of the damaged cells.
6. Transferase to protect the cells from harm.
7. Cyclase to protect the cells from harm.
8. Permeases to nourish the cells (cartilage, tendons, ligaments, organs, membranes, etc.).
9. Kinase and cyclin for cell division.
10. Polymerases to rebuild the collapsed capillaries.
11. Oxidase to support the life principle.
12. Catalase to protect the cells from hydrogen peroxide
13. GTH transferase to neutralize toxic metals.
14. Myelin polymerase to repair myelin so the axons can fire neurotransmitters.
15. GTH transferase to neutralize the halogens in pharmaceutical drugs.
16. Allosteric acid binders to neutralize acids, causing

acidosis.

17. Tissue polymerase to repair damaged tissues.

18. Hydratase to smash occlusions.

19. Superoxide dismutase to liquefy oxidants.

20. Alcohol transferase to neutralize the effect of alcohol on enzymes.

21. Reductase to smash metabolites.

22. Reductase to smash homocysteine.

23. Hydratase to enhance osmosis.

24. Lysyl oxidase to rebuild the collagen crosslinks.

25. Cytochrome c oxidase to increase the production of mitochondrial energy.

26. Hydratase to liquefy microbial toxins to stop septicemia or toxemia.

27. Hydratase to liquefy plaque and end calcifications.

28. Polymerase to rebuild the capillaries that collapsed

Considering the above, can a person who cannot produce enzymes fully recover from their illness? The answer is an emphatic no. It is the enzymes that our cells produce that clear the pathways, nourish and protect themselves from harm, help them divide, and produce neurons, neurotransmitters, hormones, etc. This is what makes the symptometric approach a natural and highly scientific one.

Pharmaceutical drugs have nothing to rebuild myelin, to allow the neural stem cells to divide and produce billions of neurons and 12 neurotransmitters. Also, they have nothing to neutralize the poisons and toxins that are in the person's blood. It is these poisons and toxins that make it impossible for the person to produce enzymes. A person who can't produce enzymes will never recover from their illnesses.

Serotonin teams up with neurons to enhance good behavior and conduct, elevate the person's mood, brighten their future, and strengthen their determination to recover. Also, neurons team up with acetylcholine to enhance learning, thinking, planning, organizing, alertness, memory, sound decision-making, etc. Can pharmaceuticals help a person produce neurons? No, they cannot.

Symptometry provides the person's cells with all the tools they need to turn their life around. Psychiatry does none of what Symptometry does.

It is the plaque in the person's midbrain, forebrain, and brain stem that causes all kinds of mental, emotional, and behavioral problems. Symptometry enables the person's cells to produce enzymes called hydratases to liquefy plaque. Psychiatric drugs never touch neurofibrillary plaque. This explains why psychiatric drugs have never stopped mental illness and will never be able to stop or prevent it.

Neurofibrillary plaque is the problem. Ischemia is the problem. Capillary collapse is the problem. Capillary occlusion is the problem. Enzyme deficit is the problem, and the non-production of enzymes is the problem, and psychiatrists leave all these problems in the person untouched.

Leaving all these problems untouched reinforces the notion that psychiatric treatment ignores the needs of the neural stem cells that produce billions of neurons, the needs of the cells in the adrenal medulla that produce epinephrine and norepinephrine, the cells in the midbrain and forebrain that produce acetylcholine and dopamine, and the cells of the brain stem that produce serotonin.

Living always requires choosing between two options. The world never had Symptometry. Now, it has it, and it is legal. Without hesitation, anyone can now choose between Symptometry and psychiatry and between psychology and Symptometry.

I am not talking about healing and treatment. These are hackneyed terms that have lost their luster and value over time. I am talking about self-love for cell self-correction, self-protection, self-cleansing, self-repair, etc. Our cells give us life, and only they can make us optimally healthy.

Also, our cells are so super-intelligent and super-smart that they can produce anything provided we know how to satisfy their needs. All we teach at the American School of Symptometry, NFP, is how to satisfy the needs of our cells. It took Symptometry 32 years to get to this point. Now, it is here. Let us make the best of it because there has never been one like it.

Chapter Fifteen
The Liver

It is said that the brain is the command center of the human body. What can the brain achieve without the liver? Nothing. What can the liver achieve without the gastrointestinal tract and the digestive glands? Nothing.

The point I am trying to make is that it is wrong to make the brain the command center without mentioning the body parts on which the brain depends to perform its multiple functions. In other words, all our organs are equally important as far as making a person healthy is concerned.

If the liver does not process oil, myelin that covers the axons will not be produced because myelin is made with lipids. Also, if the liver does not process oil, no cell will be nourished because the phospholipids that must be in the plasma membrane to allow nutrients to get into the cells and waste to exit the cell are made with oil in the liver.

Most hormones are made with non-essential amino acids and oil, and it is the liver that converts eight essential amino acids to hundreds of non-essential amino acids so hormones and neurotransmitters can be produced.

Endocrinologists claim that hormones form the

foundation of the human body. Can hormones be produced without a functioning liver? No, they cannot.

The brain and nervous systems are essential for walking, talking, thinking, driving, eating, digesting food, etc., because neurons and nerves run our body's signal system. Can neurons be produced without enzymes? No, they cannot. Can enzymes be produced without the liver? No, they cannot.

The liver, kidneys, small intestine, and large intestine are interconnected. Therefore, what happens to one will sooner or later happen to the other, and eventually, the brain will feel the impact of what happened to the organs on which it depends for supplies.

What connects all the organs? The answer is blood. It is blood that connects all the organs, membranes, tissues, etc. Therefore, no part of the body should be ischemic because if one part is ischemic and later becomes calcified, the organs and tissues that rely on the organ that is now ischemic and calcified will also become ischemic and calcified. This explains why every person who has a brain problem also has a liver problem or vice versa.

Psychiatrists and psychologists are trained to focus only on the person's brain disorders, but if the person they are treating is constipated, does not have a good appetite, cannot sleep, has a thyroid problem, a mucus membrane problem, a skin problem, etc., there is nothing they can do about these other symptoms. Why? Because these symptoms do not fall under their expertise.

Allopathic medicine is so compartmentalized this compartmentalization violates how the body is set up to function. As a result, physicians have not been trained to see a connection between a brain problem and a skin problem, the connection between a brain problem and an eye problem, a connection between a brain problem and a stomach problem, and so on.

Reflective Symptoms

The human body is interconnected in such a way that the parts of the body that can be seen reflect the concerns of the parts that cannot be seen.

For example, no one can see the liver unless with ultrasound. Since the liver is an internal organ, what does it do to draw attention to its plight? It uses the eyes, tongue, skin, cough reflex, urination (the bladder), the lumbar region (the kidneys), the rectum, the heart, the rib cage, the lungs, etc., as outlets to express its concerns. It expresses its concerns by causing the following reflective symptoms:

1. Forgetfulness
2. Attack of rage or uncontrollable anger
3. Dry lips

4. Pain in the knee
5. Cramps in the calves
6. Cramps in the toes
7. Cramps in the feet
8. Must rush to urinate, or else there will be an accident
9. Frequent belching
10. Frequent yawning
11. Varicose veins
12. Bronchitis
13. Sadness most of the day, bordering on depression
14. Discomfort felt on the right side (liver) or left side of the abdomen (spleen)
15. Jaundice with yellow conjunctiva
16. Whole skin itches
17. Rectal prolapse
18. Drooling when sleeping or excessive salivation
19. Dry feces causing constipation
20. Sciatica
21. Pain in the wrist, now called carpal tunnel syndrome
22. Sudden loose stool or diarrhea going on for days
23. Lumbago indicating congestion in the kidneys
24. Hepatitis
25. Heart pain
26. A cough attack, where the person coughs incessantly, and no amount of water or cough syrup can stop the cough
27. Coughing and spitting mucus mixed with blood
28. Pain in the ribs when coughing

29. Pain in the chest when coughing
30. Cough prevents sleep
31. Blood spitting
32. Tongue-coated white
33. Extreme fatigue after every meal
34. Frequent nosebleeds
35. Occipital headache
36. Nausea and vomiting during pregnancy, often called morning sickness
37. Little appetite or no appetite
38. Neck pain
39. Shoulder pain
40. Stomach pain no matter what is eaten.

The liver does so much that it is jammed with grime, sludge, clutter, and concretions after working 24 hours a day, seven days a week. Here comes a question. How many individuals who are now 60 years old have decongested their liver even once? It is fair to say that out of 8.9 billion inhabitants on planet Earth, maybe fewer than 3 million individuals have decongested their livers.

In Symptometry, the above-listed 40 symptoms are considered reflective symptoms because they reflect the concerns of the liver. Therefore, if the needs of the liver expressed through the above outlets are not met, the liver's condition will begin to deteriorate.

For example, when a pregnant woman suffers from morning sickness, it is considered by many cultures as normal. No, it is not normal. It is because the pregnant woman's liver problems were not addressed that she would pass them on to her baby. As a result, her baby will be born with stomach problems, food allergies and sensitivities, celiac disease, digestive problems, constipation, sugar regulation problems, skin problems, etc.

Again, the human body is interconnected, interdependent, interrelated, and integrated. No matter how hard people try to brush off this connection, it is a fact of life that must be reckoned with sooner or later.

Alpha globulins, beta globulins, and gamma globulins, as well as albumins, must always be in every organ, and the brain is no exception. Why? Because without them, the cells of organs, tissues, membranes, etc. cannot function. I will elaborate on this fact of life.

The liver produces albumins to facilitate osmosis, and it is osmosis that prevents cell dehydration. If the brain cells are dehydrated, can they divide? No, they cannot. If the neural stem cells that divide to produce billions of neurons cannot divide because they are dehydrated, can a person produce billions of neurons? No, they cannot. Hence, a connection between a calcified and malnourished liver and a dysfunctional brain that lacks neurons.

How many individuals have a dysfunctional brain because their liver cannot produce albumins? Millions. Are liver function tests useful in determining cell dehydration? No, they are not. Clinical tests have no bearing on brain disorders.

The liver produces globulins to circulate fat. If it becomes so congested that it cannot produce globulins to circulate fat out of itself, fat will accumulate in the liver, causing fatty liver and fatty degeneration of the liver. This will have serious implications on the person's brain. How? I will explain.

Fat is not supposed to be in the brain because it delays electrical signals and neuronal connectivity. Therefore, if the fatty degeneration of the liver spreads to the kidneys and the brain, the brain will atrophy, and fatty degeneration of the kidneys will cause the kidneys to malfunction.

The liver must convert eight essential amino acids to hundreds of non-essential amino acids so neurotransmitters and hormones can be produced. Then, it must convert fat to more high-density lipoprotein (good cholesterol) than low-density lipoprotein (bad cholesterol) to prevent the formation of arterial plaque, plaque psoriasis, and neurofibrillary plaque.

If the liver is massively congested, how can it do the two above-mentioned extremely important conversions? It cannot. This is the problem that every person who has a brain disorder or mental illness faces, and there is nothing that psychologists, psychiatrists, and physicians can do about it.

Can psychologists and psychiatrists ionize and degrease a congested liver so it can function normally again? No, they cannot.

Why is Symptometry stepping in to do things differently? The answer is people are tired of therapeutics that don't deliver results. In Symptometry, the proof is in the result, or the proof is in the performance.

For example, the product for liver decongestion also decongests the pharyngeal plexus to stop the cough. It decongests the neural stem cells so they can produce billions of neurons and the cells in the brain stem so they can divide to produce acetylcholine for memory. As a result, the person can feel the result of liver decongestion in no time. No wonder people all over the world are clamoring for Symptometry.

Chapter Sixteen
Cell Love

This is a new and fabulous concept that resonates well with health-conscious individuals. It does not make a person selfish but enables them to pay more attention to the needs of their cells, thereby enhancing their cells' well-being.

We did not love our cells first. They loved us first by allowing us to take a risk to be born into this world and live on this toxic planet. They produce the enzymes called kinase and cyclin to facilitate cell division and permeases to nourish our cells with water, salt, oxygen, nutrients, and oxidase to 1) facilitate gas exchange in our lungs, 2) oxygenate our blood, and 3) facilitate electron exchange in our mechanisms and systems.

Then, they produce respiratory enzymes to enable us to breathe day and night, and they allow the trophoblast to produce and position our organs, glands, membranes, sinuses, crypts, etc., where they should be so they can produce proteins to make us function automatically.

Finally, our cells produce neurons, neuropeptides, and neurotransmitters to run our brains, so we behave and conduct ourselves appropriately at home, at work, and in public, become law-abiding individuals, and contribute to the growth of the community and the expansion of the economy.

Our cells took all these measures to prove that they love us. Do we love them back? No, we don't, and this is the problem. In other words, there is tension and friction between our cells and our minds, and this is because we do not love our cells back.

All the anomalies we have are because there is tension and friction between our cells and our minds. Instead of our minds satisfying our cells' needs by eating foods that will not hurt our cells, they rather satisfy the desires of our palates, olfactory nerves, eyes, ears, and taste buds by making us eat foods and consume beverages that hurt our cells. As a result, our blood and cells are poisoned.

Our cells must have blood to function and keep us healthy in every part of our body, but the blood they are getting as a result of our bad food choices has poison in it. Either it is the poison of viruses, the poison in nuts, peaches, pears, plums, corn, etc., or the toxic acids of grapes, apples, oranges, etc., that keep hurting them and they cannot produce enzymes to neutralize them. Instead of nourishing our cells some of us are poisoning them, day after day.

Most of us are sick because we have reversed our mind/cell relationship. Instead of having a harmonious mind/cell relationship, we have a mind/cell relationship full of tension, friction, and turbulence. As a result, our cells cannot produce enzymes to do anything. Poison keeps denaturing or deactivating our enzymes.

Symptometry teaches that our first responsibility as mortals is to know the rules and regulations that govern life on planet Earth and know planet Earth as a toxic, hostile, and predatory planet.

Predators, tripwires, and boobytraps are everywhere on planet Earth. They are in hospitals, schools, homes, playgrounds, workplaces, relationships, etc. Why let our guard down? Life will be short and miserable if we continue to let our guard down.

Microbes enforce the rules of health and good hygiene. Are people aware of this fact of life about microbes? No, most of us are not because if they were, they would wash their hands before touching a fruit, and they would wash the fruit before eating it. People are not taught anything about good hygiene in schools. This is unfortunate.

Are people aware that streptococcus is always on our hands? No, most of us are not. This is why they rub their eyes with the back of their filthy hand. Streptococcus releases ten toxins, one of which can cause red eye, and another can cause a stye.

No therapeutic teaches how to live healthily on planet

Earth and restore the mind/cell harmony. Symptometry had to be invented to teach cell love and cell-based knowledge.

Most people think we were born to suffer, have diseases, and die. This is not at all why we were created. We were created and made to live on planet Earth to improve it.

To improve life on this toxic and predatory planet, we must produce neurons, neuropeptides, and neurotransmitters and not fill our midbrains, forebrains, and brain stems with neurofibrillary plaque and our arteries with arterial plaque. Most of us are completely lost and confused. This is why they are sick and suffering.

Our cells produce a symptom for a reason. It is our responsibility to find out what we did wrong that compelled our cells to produce a symptom. Instead of finding out why we produced a symptom, some individuals schedule an appointment with a physician for a diagnosis.

A diagnosis can be helpful, especially if it reveals the name of the disease. The question that a physician is not trained to answer is, what caused the disease? What did the person do wrong to compel their cells to cause a specific disease? Don't just treat the disease.

Unfortunately, this is how people have been living for thousands of years without knowing anything about the mind/cell relationship and the rules and regulations that govern life on planet Earth.

Most of us have been using the same symptom treatment method for years. Why should we expect a different result? The time for change is now, and this change comes with Symptometry and Symptometric Science.

Bibliography

Staying Healthy with Nutrition: The Complete Guide to Diet and Nutritional Medicine 21st Century Edition by Elson Haas, MD with Buck Levin, Ph.D., RD, published by Celestial Arts, ISBN 978-1-58761-179-7

Microbiology, an introduction, fifth edition, by Gerald J. Tortora, Berdell R. Funke, and Christine L. Case, published by The Benjamin/Cummings Publishing Company, Inc, ISBN 0-8053-8496-0

Hole's Human Anatomy & Physiology, seventh edition, by David Shier, Jackie Butler, and Ricki Lewis, published by WCB/McGraw Hill, ISBN 0-697-20959-0.

Index

Made in the USA
Columbia, SC
23 July 2024

39203792R00076